HEALING JOURNEYS THROUGH QUANTUM REALITIES
A HANDBOOK

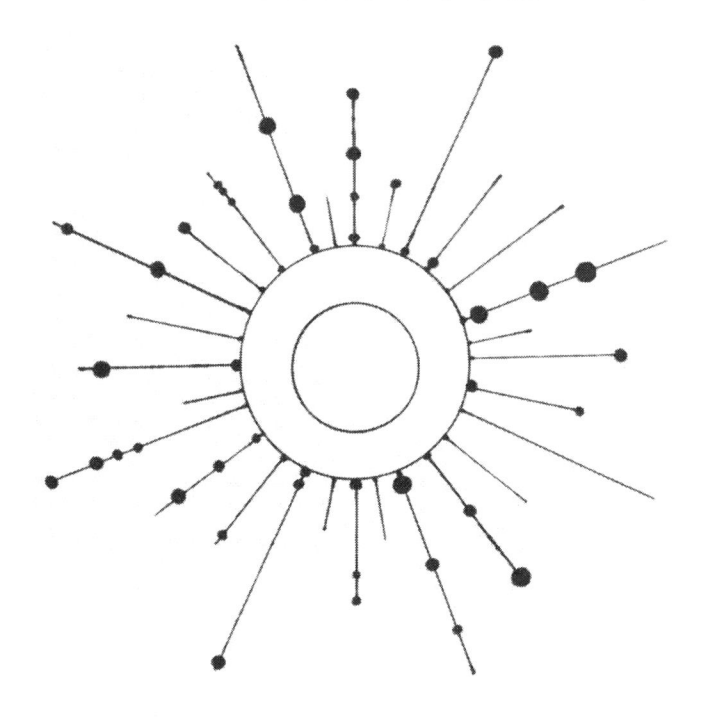

LORNA WILSON

Healing Journeys Through Quantum Realities: A Handbook
by Lorna Wilson
Copyright © 2016
All rights reserved.

This book or any portion thereof may not be reproduced or used in any manner whatsoever without the express written permission of the publisher except for the use of brief quotations in a book review.

DISCLAIMER: The information in this book does not substitute for medical care. Do not discontinue use of medication, or disregard the advice of your medical professional. This information is a supplement to any current health care treatment, and is not intended to diagnose or cure. Always consult your doctor. The author and publisher of this book are not responsible for the actions of the reader.

Cover design and interior formatting by Starfield Press
www.StarfieldPress.com

HEALING JOURNEYS
THROUGH
QUANTUM REALITIES

A HANDBOOK

CONTENTS

FOREWORD 9

INTRODUCTION 11

CHAPTER 1
PAST LIFE REGRESSION AND
QUANTUM JOURNEYS 19

CHAPTER 2
CONSCIOUSNESS EXPLORATION 35

CHAPTER 3
THE MIND AND CONSCIOUSNESS 71

CHAPTER 4
BRIDGING THE SUBCONSCIOUS
AND CONSCIOUS MIND 81

CHAPTER 5
USING YOUR BRAIN 99

CHAPTER 6
THE FACILITATOR: PUTTING YOUR HEART AND
INTENTION INTO PROVIDING THE FOUNDATION
FOR A SUCCESSFUL JOURNEY 107

CHAPTER 7
    WORKING WITH OTHERS:
    THE PRE-TALK FOUNDATION... 125

CHAPTER 8
    HYPNOTHERAPY: FACILITATING A JOURNEY 150

CHAPTER 9
    INTERWEAVING WITH THE NONPHYSICAL 225

CHAPTER 10
    DIALOGUE WITH THE SUBCONSCIOUS...................... 259

CHAPTER 11
    CLOSURE AND EXITING THE SESSION....................... 267

RECOMMENDED BOOKS 295

FOREWORD

HAVING SPENT A number of years as the Special Contributor on the Dolores Cannon Practitioner Forum helping others have successful sessions, I realised, with the passing of Dolores in 2014, that it was time for me to share my knowledge, insight, experience, and understanding about the exploration of consciousness with the general public and other healers.

Dolores Cannon was a Past Life Regression hypnotherapist and the author of 19 books documenting her sessions and insights gathered throughout her 45-year career of the multidimensional experiences of her thousands of clients, some of which reads more like science fiction. I trained with her in 2008 and had the good fortune to be selected for the class demonstration session, experiencing first-hand an empowering transformation where I met my 'others' who I have since discovered are multidimensional aspects of myself. That session was a transformative catalyst for my self-awareness as I was able to view and heal my life issues from various levels of consciousness. Although I was already a trained past-life therapist, her simple technique was powerful as it incorporated communication between the conscious, unconscious, and the subconscious mind. Adding the primary focus of the subconscious mind to the skills I have learned from numerous teachers and clients, has allowed me to simplify the process of self-exploration through inner journeys. I've been a Shamanic Practitioner, and an inquisitive researcher and explorer of consciousness, for a few decades now, and naturally incorporated what I know to be possible when interacting within the inner worlds.

Conscious exploration through journeys into quantum realities is a gentle yet powerful process, which uses our natural mind-states to engage inwardly, with the 'imaginal' or 'shamanic' realms, the realms of the imagination, in simple and effective ways. Through such explorations it is possible, within our individual expanded awareness, to come to a direct experience of personal wisdom and growth; as we expand our awareness we make changes in line with that.

Whether you are a curious armchair consciousness researcher, or an active participant in venturing into the multidimensional worlds, there will be something of interest within these pages for everyone. Once you have mastered some of the basic fundamentals contained within this book, you will have enough in your toolbox to explore with more confidence. Indeed, there is room for creative flexibility within the ideas shared here.

INTRODUCTION

"Quantum healing is healing the bodymind from a quantum level. That means from a level which is not manifest at a sensory level. Our bodies ultimately are fields of information, intelligence and energy. Quantum healing involves a shift in the fields of energy information, so as to bring about a correction in an idea that has gone wrong. So quantum healing involves healing one mode of consciousness, mind, to bring about changes in another mode of consciousness, body." —Deepak Chopra

*H*EALING JOURNEYS THROUGH *Quantum Realities* is a handbook to demystify the process of facilitating hypnotic self-exploration, using revelations from the subconscious mind. These ideas will be shared from my experiences; experiences that are continually evolving as I learn something new, which frequently happens. To do this, I've tried to demonstrate the skeletal structure as the foundation of understanding in order to facilitate an inner journey while leaving enough room for you to launch your own creative form.

As we change genetic patterns we move into a new

era of self-revelation and healing past trauma. *Healing Journeys through Quantum Realities* encompasses vibrational energy healing, cognitive behavioural change, soul retrieval, remote viewing, past life regression, shamanism, channelling, out-of-body experiences, and every type of inner self-exploration. Our outer waking awareness is primarily focused on our external everyday life or the surface layers of our consciousness, while our inner non-ordinary states of consciousness are comprised of an intuitive knowing expressed through our spiritual or higher states of consciousness. As more discoveries are made about the cosmos and our connection with it, science fiction is eventually becoming a reality that more of us can readily accept.

Many of us are seeking answers and ways in which we can be more accepting of ourselves and comfortable in our own skins. We are inspired to go beyond ourselves to find more self-love and inner happiness. There are ideas in this book that will help show the way to understand and unravel your personal inner mysteries, discover why your life is as it is, and heal, simply by extending your physical awareness into the nonphysical to access your soul's wisdom.

When we journey into our inner world we experience the unusual that is no different from when in our dream world, where we have quite bizarre interactions with dream characters that on analysis has symbolic or direct meaning, adding to our capability of aiding in our self-discoveries. When personal transformation occurs it results in self-integration and when utilising our subconscious resources this can occur quite rapidly.

This handbook is a guide to facilitate a journey into the quantum possibilities of our human potential, presented interactively with other multiple layers of consciousness and intelligence. You may even discover that there is a subtle energetic effect on you, the reader, as spontaneous thoughts, associations or realisations intuitively arise from your subconscious. The information is multi-layered with actionable and experiential ideas or techniques that will appeal to both practitioner and consciousness explorer alike. It is my hope that the information within this handbook will give you an in-depth understanding of the simplicity of inner journeying, what transpires during an inner adventure, and how to facilitate such a journey for others. This is all explained and demonstrated through the session stories.

Quantum physics is proving that everything is energy, that everything has a vibrational frequency, and that our thoughts are expressed as an energetic stimuli inside the brain, yet still consciousness itself does not need the brain and is active even when the brain is dead. Our brain cells, or neurons, communicate with each other through electrical signals, which are measurable as brain wave patterns. Our body is primarily water, which is very significant for efficient brain activity and the production of neurotransmission. From the research and water experiments of the late Dr. Masaru Emoto we discover that the power of our thoughts can affect the quality of water, creating molecular changes in its structure and harmonics. We can take this a step further, applying this to the physical body and imagine how the potential of our thoughts will impact its structure. We can literally and authentically change our feelings by changing our minds—our thoughts. Not only do our thoughts affect our feelings, but our feelings determine the quality of our thoughts. Our feelings are often stimulated by external things that happen to us and our perception of them, what others say or do, or how we would have liked the outcome of particular situations to have been. Our thoughts are what we base those perceptions or 'memories' on, even though we often confuse the two by thinking that our feelings stem from our thoughts, which they can as we create our internal repetitive dialogue. The paradox is that we can have feelings that are not founded on our thoughts, but on our beliefs about our feelings. Our body, however, remembers everything accurately and a bridge can be used to access the stories that are held within its cellular structure. New neural pathways, literally the physical matrix of thought patterns, are created by the new insights experienced during the process of hypnosis. The witnessing consciousness has a new discovery. The body changes accordingly. These changes move the mind and body beyond old comfort zones, into an expanded awareness and an increased vibrational frequency, freeing the mind from the past and creating an evolution in self-awareness. These changes are the natural outcome of any inner exploration. It is an easy way to gain insight painlessly and effect immediate and lasting changes.

New methods of scientific discoveries of consciousness which are constantly being discovered, still only barely touch the surface of our true human potential or capabilities. Deeper personal exploration is up to us, the individual, to enable our own personal growth as we continue to evolve in self-understanding. There is a sense that the entirety of the self contains vast potential, potential we are hardly aware of, and in many ways we can barely imagine. Something, however, nudges us from deep within, making us yearn for greater self-awareness. Our longing for a more personal, direct connection with who we are, with clarity of our life's purpose, with increased self-knowledge—this longing itself fuels our transformational experiences. Any external searching for answers eventually leads us to look deeply within, to resolve personal conflicts, to embrace ourselves beyond inner conflict and self-doubt.

We are led into ever-unfolding layers of insight into our emotional conflicts and ever-evolving expansions and deepening of self-compassion. Through journeying into quantum realities we can eventually move beyond all concepts, thoughts, and ideas, into a direct experience of our spiritual essence, into a direct experience of the fundamental and ultimately indestructible wholeness of the soul. When we discover other parts of ourselves we benefit by integrating their skills and insights as we become more consciously aware.

Throughout these pages I will speak collectively of the SC, so as to represent the totality of the sub- or unconscious mind. There are many different kinds of maps available to uncover what is in our subconscious, and many ways to explore otherwise hidden terrains—such as out-of-body experiences, lucid dreaming, talk therapies, plant medicines and hypnosis. The map into quantum realities is created by your own unconscious mind that involves a journey inward. When exploring the SC, we can gain unlimited access to all that pertains to our own well-being. It helps to understand how to use the map and how to manoeuvre within it, without leading or judging the experience.

No preconceived location needs to be suggested or

forced. Instead, allow the SC to take the lead and reveal whatever information is most pertinent and relevant to what is going on in the conscious mind of the client. The SC will automatically locate whatever needs to be rebalanced, or it will show scenes to impress, suggest or initiate areas in need of change.

During the hypnosis portion of the session the facilitator's role is like that of a tour guide who assists the client in exploring their consciousness. Here the facilitator is in the role of an open-minded journalist who has a casual, accepting curiosity of the unknown without prejudice. To do this we must develop good communication skills that enable us to match the varied levels of understanding and the differing levels of comfort zones of each client. Staying open and receptive is important so that we, as facilitators, do not think we know more than the client's own SC. When we have constrictive viewpoints we lose sight of the larger picture. Consciousness cannot be boxed into any one concept, as we are continually evolving and changing our minds about our personal reality. The practitioner's role is to stay grounded, attuned with the Divine, making no assumptions, and asking pertinent questions ending or beginning conceptually with, "If that is appropriate, or relevant."

Quantum journeys invites you to journey into the vast, open expansiveness of your mind. It enables you to have direct experiences through your soul's history, where you may even experience consciousness as other life forms, both on and off this planet. It allows you to experience consciousness as nature, colour, sound, atmosphere, pure energy or virtually any sentient life form that exists within the awareness of consciousness.

After having such experiences we can no longer pretend that nature is not alive, or that colour is not interactive, self-aware or has a vibrational frequency. Also, it is not quite accurate to think of this therapy as a regression—which suggests a backward movement. In truth, collective information is found in a 360-degree range of all possible, multidimensional realities.

Finally, it's important to remember that personal transformation is a self-initiated process. In other words, by choosing to have a journey of exploration through hypnosis, we are consciously choosing to increase our self-integration. Furthermore, we are consciously choosing to utilise our subconscious resources in order to do so. This means that change is self-driven and comes from the client. The hypnotherapist is merely a guide on (or facilitator of) the journey.

~

I am truly indebted to all of the many clients who have shared so much wisdom with me from their higher conscious mind. Each of your sessions were the equivalent of having classes on spirituality and conscious living. I am forever grateful for the trust you bestowed on me, when allowing me to peek into your life.

My deepest gratitude to Jacqueline Harvey for helping me to cross my t's and dot my i's. I was deeply honored by the following practitioners who may not have known how much they inspired me to complete this handbook. Without your encouragement, and insistence, I may never have put my thoughts to paper.

Adriyana Hodge
DimensionalJourneys.com

Angela Rose Pate
AccesSpirit.com

Anne Ashley Jones
anneashleyjones@hotmail.com

Marilyn Brady
TappingTherapyPlus.com

Suzanne Kahn
SuzanneKahn.com

Clare Joslin
Alohaclinic-QHHT.org

CHAPTER 1

PAST LIFE REGRESSION AND QUANTUM JOURNEYS

Past Life Research

"*Every part of the body, it would seem, has in one person or another revealed some old accident or wound. But Past Life traumas always have a specific and not a general relationship to the current physical problem...*" — Roger Woolger Ph.D.

PAST LIFE INVESTIGATION consists of practice- and evidence-based approaches. Practice-based research uses results from pre- and post-therapy questionnaires, using large numbers of clients with a range of problems. Evidence-based research works with a group of clients with the same issue, to demonstrate its effectiveness or not in that area.

In practice-based past life research, Hazel Denning studied the results of eight regression therapists and over 1000 clients, between 1985 and 1992. The results were measured just after the therapy, then after six months, a year, two years and five years. Of the 450 clients who could still be tracked after five years: 24% reported the symptoms had completely gone, 23% reported considerable or dramatic improvement, and 17% reported a noticeable improvement (TanDam, 1990).

Dr. Heather Rivera (2012) worked with 180 clients from a wide range of religious backgrounds and showed that, apart from the therapeutic benefits: 74% found their life was more meaningful, and 80% found death no longer held any fear.

In evidence-based past life research, Ron Van der Maesen (1999) worked with 54 clients who had recurrent disturbing voices or thoughts. Six months after the therapy an external psychiatrist studied the results: 25% found the voices disappeared, and 32% could now cope with the issue. Overall, 80% had a positive subjective experience and would recommend past life therapy to others with a similar problem.

Ron Van der Maesen (1998) also conducted past life research with Tourette's syndrome. This is a disorder characterised by involuntary, repetitive behaviour. The current view is that this is usually a life-long condition. The work was conducted with 22 clients aged from 9 to 52 years. Of the ten subjects who completed the therapy and responded to the follow-up questionnaire a year later, 50% reported that their motor tics had largely disappeared or been greatly reduced in frequency. The same also applied to their vocal tics. Five also reported that they were free of medication, in sharp contrast to the pre-study period.

Returning to practice-based past life research, Wambach (Snow, 1986) conducted the largest study using 26 regression therapists who had worked with a total of 17,350 clients. Of these, 63% reported an improvement in physical symptoms, and 40% reported an improvement in their interpersonal relationships.

References:

Freeman T. B. (1997) 'Past Life and Inter-life Reports of Phobic People: Patterns and Outcome', *The Journal of Regression Therapy*, Volume XI (1), International Association for Regression Research and Therapies

Snow C. (1986) 'Past Life Therapy: The Experiences of Twenty-Six Therapists', *The Journal of Regression Therapy*, Volume I (2)

Denning H. (1987) 'The Restoration of Health Through Hypnosis', *Journal of Regression Therapy* 2:1, pp. 524.

Rivera H. (2012) 'Measuring the Therapeutic Effects of Past Life Regression', *The Journal of Regression Therapy*, International Association for Regression Research and Therapies. Also see **www.plrinstitute.org**

Van der Maesen R. (1998) 'Past Life Therapy for Giles De La Tourette's Syndrome', *The Journal of Regression Therapy*, Volume XII (1), International Association for Regression Research and Therapies

Van der Maesen R. (1999) 'Past Life Therapy for People Who Hallucinate Voices', *The Journal of Regression Therapy*, Volume XIII (1), International Association for Regression Research and Therapies - Andy Tomlinson; The Past Life Regression Academy

Regression Therapy and Quantum Hypnosis

Regression therapy is used primarily to access past events or lives. Understanding a previous existence or 'past life' is not a critical element to make quantum shifts in awareness. Past lives can be fun and helpful, but our focus is to access the larger essence of the individual.

A primary difference between a past life regression and a quantum journey is that the latter includes direct communication with one's multidimensional 'realities', which is derived from an inner exploration of consciousness expansion. Universal experiences through the interaction with other aspects of self, knowledge and insights are frequently reported and may include past life stories, but are not dependent as the underpinning of the session.

To incorporate the total person holistically we must include these spiritual aspects as well, because we operate and exist on multidimensional levels. Quantum journeys move beyond traditional past life therapy, as we enter into quantum fields of reality and into the psychology of the universe, we explore its direct effects upon us. These fields are what we identify as spiritual realms, for lack of a more accurate description.

> *"Self exploration can require courage... it can take you to and thru some really interesting places... Vortices, sanctums, deep astral inner space, various states of Being, of Is-Ness. It's pretty cool stuff, the interior journey following the energy where it leads you... And not without perils, not without perils... It can lead you into some pretty hairy places, to places where the piece of others, albeit well-*

meaning are unbeknownst to both of you feeding off your light...It can lead you through shamanic extractions, "past lives", and the lifting and shifting of the stories of the trauma patterns of humanity which are imprinted on your DNA... And if you find your way through all of it, it can lead you to the forgotten or as-yet-undiscovered roots of your own wholeness... It can lead you to your Self."
—Murshida VA

Quantum Journeys Defined

Quantum Journeys is a method of self exploration that works at the quantum or a subatomic depth of consciousness, and is directed by the higher conscious levels of the mind, or the soul. The subconscious mind knows what to reveal to each individual, on any topic of relevance from its wealth of knowledge and wisdom. This becomes accessible through an expansion of consciousness, or entering what was formerly identified as an altered state, that differs from the everyday waking consciousness. We now know that these altered states are natural phenomenon known as measurable brainwave states.

Journeys are Shamanic

Quantum journeys are a way to have mystical experiences, and receive spiritual teachings communicated through self-interactive experiences. Shamanism involves utilising altered states of consciousness accessed through the different states of brainwave patterns, to interact with the spiritual, unseen world. In shamanic beliefs there are three worlds, which I'll simplify as the Lower World of the subconscious, the Middle World, which is parallel to our physical one, and the Upper World of the higher consciousness. Soul retrieval through the understanding of soul loss, or with the need for removal of toxic energy intrusions are known as an Extraction process. It was natural to be guided to use all of my knowledge and training to facilitate others in doing these things for themselves when, or if necessary. Opportunities would arise in unexpected ways to push me creatively to find solutions or spontaneously rewrite a script or change the routine. Soul retrieval became reintegration of the fragmented self, or reclaiming the energy of things that made us shut down emotionally. Clearing energy fields, becoming grounded, feeling optimistic, calm and clear can be what happens after the removal of intrusive, draining elements.

The very act of experiencing yourself as an immortal being existing completely independent from your physical body, often removes the fear of death, while allowing for a direct experience with the non-physical. Consciousness explorers having experienced their consciousness as separate from the body, know without doubt that they do not die for although the atomic structure of the body dies, consciousness lives on. One of the benefits of a past life regression is the direct knowing of this after going through a personal death scene. With tragic and painful deaths the client often describes exiting the body prior to its death and watching the dying body from afar. With NDE's people describe not feeling the pain of the hurt body once they 'die' and are no longer confined to it until after they have been resuscitated and are back in their body. It is only once their consciousness is encased within the body that they feel the physical cause that had projected them out of it.

With the discovery that it is possible to change genetic patterns, we have moved into a new era of self-revelation; it is now possible to heal trauma through the efforts of the mind. In the new science of epigenetics, cell biologist Bruce Lipton, Ph.D., the author of *The Biology of Belief: Unleashing the Power of Consciousness, Matter & Miracles* demonstrates how it's not our genes and DNA that controls our biology but our thoughts. He has this to say about the power of our thoughts:

> *"The Wisdom of Your Cells is a new biology that will profoundly change civilization and the world we live in. This new biology takes us from the belief that we are victims of our genes, that we are biochemical machines, that life is out of our control, into another reality, a reality where our thoughts, beliefs and mind control our genes, our behavior and the life we experience. This biology is based on current, modern science with some new perceptions added.*
>
> *"The new science takes us from victim to creator; we are very powerful in creating and unfolding the lives that we lead. This is actually knowledge of self and if we understand the old axiom, "Knowledge is power," then what we are really beginning to understand is the knowledge of self-power. This is what I think we will get from understanding the new biology."*

There are techniques within this book that will help you understand how our physical awareness extends to travel into other dimensions or realities. Personal transformation in hypnosis occurs firstly through the self-initiated choice to have a session to experience in-depth insights for personal growth through utilising our subconscious resources.

The format for Quantum Journeys is a simple, three-part process, that is not restricted by any cultural, generational, race or any particular topic of enquiry through self-exploration of the individual mind.

Pre-talk = Communication with the conscious mind.

Hypnosis = Revelation from the subconscious mind.

HS (higher self/mind) dialogue = Communication and resolution through the higher consciousness levels of the mind.

If it is something that is within the mind or thoughts then it is worth exploring the whys, or the how's. The answers and knowledge comes from you and you will have the direct experience of this personal knowing. The pre-talk interview is where the communication stems from the conscious mind to map the starting point of inquiry to begin identifying the desired outcome. Dialoguing with the higher self allows for communication with the parts of the mind that knows the answers and will begin healing when necessary. Hypnosis or deep relaxation will reveal the identifying causes or connections in the subconscious mind and show the original cause, which may be metaphorical, an analogy or even a past life. Whatever the unconscious mind expresses will always be relevant and may include the direct cause or antidote.

Some of my best teachers were the 'ordinary' client with no particular spiritual beliefs or agenda. This session is a great example of the contrasts between our conscious beliefs, and our subconscious metaphorical use of symbolic details. It was a bit difficult to condense this session to the bare essentials but I have tried to leave it as verbatim as possible. Throughout the whole session, this client was talking back and forth from different levels of awareness, often filled with disbelief as a 'Christian.' Sometimes she spoke slowly, but at other times very fast and knowledgeable. She experienced a wide range of emotions that spanned from utter disbelief, to hilarious outbursts of laughter. She came for a session as she was feeling stuck in her life but was afraid of leaving her job security.

When asked to go to her beautiful place to begin the session, she had found herself near a waterfall. At the waterfall, she had become aware of rocks and at the same time began to 'feel stuck.' Using that feeling as a bridge we managed to discover that she has a fear of heights that we were successful in moving her through. (Whenever fear shows up it must be faced and released.) Once she overcame her fear, which was described as an 'initiation challenge', she was then able to move forward, which led her to her 'group' that she affectionately recognised as 'The Jumpers.' They were all having a fun and joyful time jumping off rocks where she happily joined them. No longer fearful, now feeling completely at ease, she climbed up the rocks and playfully jumped off numerous times with her friends. She had transitioned from fear to happiness. Both she and they jumped around a lot. The only requirement was to identify herself as a jumper and she accomplished this by moving beyond fear, and jumping.

'The jumpers' are risk takers. Their nature is to take risks of all kinds, which creates an innate state of fearlessness. If you jump, you are fearless. There are no age restrictions to this activity or ability. These are people who dare. The group of jumpers do not recruit others, nor do they look for new people to join them. Seekers find them. That is how it works. No conscious doing or seeking is needed on our part. It is the end result of our actions that lead us to 'them.' We cannot find or join them through willpower. (This is all leading up to those who will make the shift.) Jumping IS love and jumpers ARE love. As jumpers, we can break through the un-loveable.

Within the galaxy there are many stars connected to our 'expansion' — through our magnetic fields. There is a loud 'hallelujah' echoing through the cosmos each time an entity embraces a major shift like this. There is a lot of power being passed on to us via our electromagnetic fields. Our body fields are changing and this cosmic power is influencing lots of 'stuff' that we may not be consciously aware of. Time is shifting and the electromagnetic field is connected to time shifting. The jumpers are waiting and rooting for all of us to jump.

Meanwhile, the jumpers continued talking with the client about a shift that is occurring, and she peppered the entire dialogue with, "I don't know what I'm saying, and this is crazy, but... I'm a Christian... what do they mean?" Those who are in fear are not able to shift, but those who have overcome their fears will have no problem embracing the shift. Those who can't shift will simply go to another dimension. The shift occurs for those who are fearless because they have already made the jump, so to speak, by having been diligent in their own preparation. They have already been opened up and responded to the import of this message.

We're getting ready for a collective shift. "Those who have fears and choose to keep being the way they are,

are going to have a lot of problems with that. Those who have been going from 'here' to 'there' are ready for the shifting because they are made aware of the shifting, and me just being here in this session, I am ready for it. We'll find each other to facilitate the shifting."

As we progressed through the session, the client suddenly said, "I'm talking about this very confidentially because I know, in a very weird way, that a lot of power is coming into us and being given to those who are embracing the shift and that we are being given the help we need. There's a need for those who can receive it because those who will accept it will know that it is close to coming and it is a de-materialising, which means 'transcending', and one happens to allow the other. I am one of the influencers of people and events. I do not influence through judgments, but by thoughts and inner knowing. It's going to happen and it's going to happen fast, and I'm saying that I don't want to go around like a headless chicken and they say that a lot of people are being raised to be fearful of supernatural things but not the worldly things. It's not how strong you are, it's more about the things that can't be seen. We need to be ready to jump first with our hearts, and to be fearless. You can jump and when you do you will no longer be fearful. Strength isn't the key, desire is. Just being in touch with who you are and having the desire to be yourself will influence things, as it is who you are that is most important. Ask for more help and you will meet more like-minded people so that you can grow and be at ease. People are waiting for you... There's a wonderful world out there. It's time. A lot of things have to do with timing. When it's time, it's time. Everything is perfect."

The client goes on to share that, "No one needs to do anything but be aware of the shifting. Just embrace it. You will know when it is taking place, it will not be unknown. When you feel it, you will know. Some people will know but will not understand it and so they will have resistance. We will go to a higher level, a dimension that is open now for us to access. It is a given. We don't have to know anything, just embrace it, and the gifts of knowing and doing will come naturally, like abilities that can influence material things. It's a given. We don't have to earn it, just embrace it. People who are bound by their securities won't be able to access it (the shift). If you are not bound by your securities then you will be able to shift.

"You don't know how many lives you are living while you are living here. How we are living here is not always exciting, but we are having excitement elsewhere...and eventually it catches up with us. It's other dimensional living that is being experienced differently than what we know here, and whatever is happening there can happen here. It's interchangeable depending on where we want to be. It's like peeking into 'there' from 'here.'..because we can transfer skills from one dimension to the other."

Empaths

Gina came for a session as she felt too sensitive to the energy of others, which often left her very tired or feeling quite drained. During her session we were told that "it is designed" that there are more empaths on the planet at this time now because we are becoming more consciously aware that all of life is sentient and are conscious beings in their own right. There is a need for humanity to become more sensitive to nature if the planet is to survive and thrive. This sensitivity also opens up the awareness of a cosmic connection to other planets and their possible living beings.

When speaking from her higher level of awareness she had this to say about what it really means to be an empath:

"Being empathic, we are able to find common ground with everyone we come across, but we must also understand that they are not necessarily the same energy as us. We must maintain our own frequency, by taking the time to be in solitude, or breathing deeply. If we close our eyes and focus we will sense the interaction of the energy fields to see how to interact with the other person. It is time to use that empathic ability that has brought so many so much sadness and misery (from being oversensitive to the depleting energy of others). Empaths have not realised that it allows them to connect with, and, feel every living aspect of the planet. When they breathe deeply they can expand this connection and awareness to the place (within themselves) that they would choose to be in. It is under their control, although they may not realise this, and see it as scattering their energy, when in fact it is a most prized position to have. Used correctly, they must learn to distance themselves from those who do not benefit their highest good. There is much blessings in being an empath, as they can access the consciousness of everything and anything, from a plant to an insect or to whole star systems and galaxies. When empaths join forces their power becomes magnified, and they are able to fully integrate the higher dimensions into this planet. Working together makes it the paradise it was designed to be or dreamed of."

Individuals who consider themselves empaths in their day-to-day life will benefit by grounding themselves before working with others, so that they are not in a state of consciousness where they are enmeshing their own energy with that of others or allowing it to happen unconsciously. Should that happen, it generally has a strong impact that can feel especially draining. This is not what is involved when working as a surrogate for the healing of another person. It is our consciousness that accesses consciousness through the filter or software programming of another, to locate information about the questions asked. It is not our physical personality at work; it is our higher collective consciousness that is already connected to the totality of humanity.

Surrogates

All energy is a vibrational frequency and consciousness is non-local fields of information. A surrogate can therefore access the information of others by energetically tapping into their energy fields—this is known in shamanism as 'entering the landscape' of another person. In a less deep way we can enter this reality through the conscious mind, by feeling empathy and imagining 'as if' we were experiencing life through the filter of another; this form of empathy uses the mental, subtle body. However, during hypnosis or any altered state, we can physically experience what the other person feels through the direct contact of their personal fields. We do not possess them, but we can see or view the world from their unique perspective, by simply engaging with an energy duplicate of them. We do not transfer our energy in any way. We simply access the information held in their matrix or energy field.

When undergoing surrogate work we assist with healing, through understanding what is occurring in the person we are helping. This is no different from using our state of consciousness to see through the eyes of another; this is simply another form of remote spiritual healing. Most importantly, during the pre-talk, we would have explored gently and subtly what investment the client may have in not healing. It is best to first investigate a 'diagnosis' of what approach to undertake, e.g is the problem, emotional, or purely physical, what is the best path for healing, etc. We can explore why they are not healing, and can discover the deeper meaning behind the problem or disease, and any possible solutions advisable. Sometimes, an immediate healing takes place miraculously. Miraculously, as we cannot determine beforehand who is able to heal permanently, why some people and not others, or the souls destined reason for maintaining an illness.

CHAPTER 2

CONSCIOUSNESS EXPLORATION

> *"The Akashic Records might seem to be some heavenly office room filled with file cabinets. Akasha, however, means 'space.' The 'records' implied are intrinsic to the oneness of infinite consciousness. They are called so because it's possible to access any specific part of omniscience you wish."*
> —Ervin László. *The Akashic Experience: Science and the Cosmic Memory Field*

ALL GOOD STORIES have a beginning, middle and end. They are each different in tempo, action and flow, allowing the mind to expand and take from it a personal meaning. A session that journeys into quantum realities is no different. In a healing session the pre-talk uses the client's conscious mind, and is underpinned with emotional concerns, maybe dissatisfaction in life and the hope for desired changes to manifest. All life experiences are subjective in nature, and cannot be completely understood by anyone other than our own inner self. Our history can be accessed, karma can be understood and rebalanced, and physical healing can occur by revealing and removing the original triggers, while initiating alchemical processes within the body. The physical and metaphysical are intertwined, and we can explore our consciousness by inner journeying into quantum, multidimensional realities.

Subjective emotional life stories are repeatedly reprogrammed into our thinking through unconscious patterns that the conscious mind has no awareness of. There are many core beliefs buried within the subconscious mind that are self defeating, and, until change takes place at this core level, permanent resolution may be delayed. Old ingrained habits and thinking patterns may reappear in moments of stress or low-level moods as our weakest points become triggered. It is human nature to fall back into old, familiar thinking patterns and when this happens it depletes our energy. It's important to thoroughly explore the underlying causes and the purpose that the 'problems' served, and then transforming them into better more comfortable feelings. Discovering this information can be enormously helpful, as it opens the door to releasing the original cause, providing deep insight and self awareness.

Many people don't believe they can access their own inner world, but I'm going to share with you a way in which you can connect to your spiritual essence, or assist others in doing so. This essence has many labels: higher self, soul, spirit, source, the Akashic field or collective consciousness. As multidimensional energy ourselves, it's necessary that we move beyond all labels and release the confinement of limitations.

Consciousness exploration through journeys into quantum realities is a gentle yet powerful process, which uses our natural mind-states to engage in a process that is simple and effective. Through such explorations within our individual expanded awareness comes a direct experience of personal wisdom and growth.

Contained within our own histories are a variety of lifetimes and experiences—they could be planetary, sacred, philosophical, historical, cosmic or Extra Terrestrial based—it doesn't matter what the mind reveals, because it will be natural and relevant to the receiver. Soul aspects inhabiting different timelines or life forms often show up in a session and are accepted naturally by the client while in a trance state. Having prepared the client to become curious about what is within their own subconscious, we can encourage them to prepare for any eventuality that may occur. Our manner with the client should be calm, empathetic, light-hearted and encompassing all that is necessary to create a 'yes' mind-set, in order to induce an integrative expansion of consciousness.

When clients return to full consciousness they often question if they have made up their experience. The journey may have revealed things that are far removed from what the conscious mind believes possible. So it's always important to discover what these experiences will mean to the client and what the higher self is trying to convey.

I encourage clients to notice how the information

revealed has answered their questions—and how the subconscious mind has responded to their needs for increases in life potential. Once the information surfaces during the session it will continue to reveal deeper levels of understanding about the self over time. As the dots continue to connect, the client becomes able to make sense of things that were previously unknown or misunderstood. Also, we sometimes receive information that will only make sense later on. Our spiritual essence has faith in our evolutionary growth, and is always busy laying the groundwork for future realisations.

After doing this work for a few decades I have noticed that the subconscious (SC) has never used the term 'dimensions' during inward exploration; it is we who use labels for what we cannot otherwise define or explain. Exploration of our inner world moves us beyond limiting parameters of what we previously perceived as physical reality. We may experience different timelines—such as those in the past, present or future—but the mind itself is not confined by time or space. It follows streams of creativity that reach far beyond the conscious mind's ability to truly know, or define. Without having direct experiences and anchoring them into awareness, we are left with limiting beliefs and knowledge.

The conscious mind, being only physically perceptive, thinks if it cannot see tangible things with physical eyes then they are not real. When we are asleep and involved with our dreams the conscious mind is absent, and on waking up it accepts most dream imagery as unusual. Acceptance of what occurs in a journey of the unusual is important to discover the deeper meanings within. If we encourage clients to dismiss ideas of what they think of as real and unreal, and encourage them to simply allow impressions to reveal themselves, they will discover they can explore without any self-imposed restrictions, and the quality of information improves. To become a consciousness explorer we have to become curious. Suspension of any belief about how things should be gives the client permission to be expansive. Without that expansion, accessing higher knowledge and wisdom becomes limited to the framework of our beliefs.

Multifaceted Awareness

Sometimes clients think the communication with their SC is something other than different aspects of themselves, not realising that they have within them a range or levels of consciousness all functioning concurrently. Our eyes are constantly taking in peripheral information, even if they are focused on what is in front of them. I point out to clients that even though they are focused on me, their subconscious is taking in all the information within the room as we naturally multi-task with our awareness. It helps to remind them how multi-faceted we all are, and that we consciously multi-task all the time. For example, we can listen to the TV, talk to the kids, think about what to cook for dinner, look outside the window and be on the phone all at the same time. In other words, our ability to be aware on many levels at the same time is what allows us to realise that our consciousness is capable of much more than simple one-dimensional awareness. Likewise, our higher self or SC retains and reflects other facets of ourselves, or higher more creative states of consciousness that come forward when the right and left hemispheres of our brains are working together harmoniously. This happens naturally when we are relaxed or daydreaming. Explaining this to clients during the pre-talk relieves them of any pressure about thinking that someone or something other than themselves is going to come to their rescue or make them lose control.

Clients regularly experience cosmic interactions with other beings, aspects of themselves and uncover sacred, metaphysical and historical content, as they tap into their own personal histories. When accessing experiences as an 'alien' life form, or even as a plant or a rock, they are spoken of in a very natural and easy way without discrimination.

Spiritual Abilities

As humans we all have a wide range of spiritual abilities designed to enable us to access non-physical information that we cannot see with our five bodily senses. However, our basic senses can be expanded and strengthened to reach far beyond what we currently perceive as ordinary reality. In effect, we can choose to expand our own reality at will.

Our primary senses can be elevated and expanded, in order to interact comfortably with various fields and frequencies of intelligent awareness. When we use our senses in a non-physical way, seeing becomes clairvoyance, hearing becomes clairaudience, feeling becomes clairsentience and smelling is called clairscent. These inner senses are not just limited to psychics or mediums, as we all use them through imagination, memories or our intuition. As we develop, strengthen and trust our inter-dimensional senses a whole new world of possibilities arises, emerges and opens up within us. The impressions we perceive while in a more inclusive and expansive state of awareness are witnessed by the mind's eye, and can be experienced as a direct knowing and spontaneous thought or realisations.

If someone wants to explore his or her inner awareness, then regression therapy is beneficial. Clinical studies have proved that past life regression therapy has profound psychosomatic results in finding the original cause of physical disease, and is beneficial for a variety of mental disturbances or psychological discomforts. As a therapy, quantum journeying allows us to disengage from our outer life, allowing our subconscious to bring to the forefront of our mind a 'story' that emotionally matches what we are externally experiencing. Imagine that you can participate in a spontaneously created subconscious revelation, where the answers you seek surface to the forefront of your awareness without you knowing how or what will be shown next. The stories unfold bit by bit — and are never what we expect — so it is helpful to be curious, whether as an observer or participant, and to expect the unexpected.

We experience this in a similar way when daydreaming, or when dreaming while sleeping. In our dreams we often experience a wide range of unexpected and symbolic events, and often spend time later trying to decipher them. When experiencing a past life memory it can easily be deciphered, as it becomes instantly self-explanatory. Not only do we experience them as real, but also we feel the emotions and sense the connections to previous events in our life and formative years. Quite often, after such an experience, we feel the truth for ourselves and sense a greater connection to our spiritual essence.

During our dreams or daydreams we don't question the imagery and experiences that our consciousness interacts with, although we may later think of them as fantasy. It is no different when accessing our inner reality through quantum journeying as that may be similar in symbolism to our dreamscape.

These life memories are not always completely accurate, as they are based on the perception of the experiencer and may only be true to the individual. But this is what is important, as our subconscious is revealing what is buried beneath our conscious awareness. The emotional impact is subjective and relevant to whatever questions we may have. One example is a client who thought his mother didn't love him; this was re-experienced from different angles during the session, showing that his mother did love him as much as she was capable of in relation to other things that were going on in her life and mind.

Memories

Everything is as we perceive it to be. Memories are often emotional perceptions that are not necessarily true or accurate. As an example, many people remember the same event quite differently. When a person shifts their perception then the energy that was holding it in place is released and healing can occur. I think of our life experiences as stories that are subjective in nature; we must find our own understanding experience and meaning in all memories. Asking for or intentionally guiding a shift in perception leaves it up to the client to express another way that things could have been, or can now be, viewed.

Our conscious mind rationalises things and files them away into specific categories, such as, 'I liked this,' or 'I didn't like that,' and at the moment of the original cause or emotive decision we slip into a hypnotic trance state. In fact, any time we experience an emotion we enter into a trance state of sorts. When we want to rethink something, we have to go back into that trance state to experience the emotions that led us to believe whatever it is we came to believe.

As we close our eyes while thinking of certain memories, we can ask ourselves, 'Where is that emotion felt in the body, and what does it feel like?'

As we guide clients to follow this process and describe how it feels, it is common to hear such responses as, "The emotions feel trapped or stuck in this or that place... It feels, tense, tight, a pressure, an aching, stabbing feeling etc." In order to release such feelings we have to go back into the memory to view it from a larger perspective. We are fully capable of doing this for ourselves, independent of another person's assistance, although as a therapist you can help clients to achieve what they may feel reluctant to face on their own.

Hypnotic fractionation is a process that through opening and closing the eyes allows for a deepening process with each eye closure and works subtly and effortlessly. There's the added benefit of confirming the client's levels of suggestibility to follow your directions. It was originally discovered that when clients came repeatedly for additional sessions, they went deeper into trance. One hypnosis pioneer thought opening and closing the eyes during a single session might produce the same results and it turned out he was right. So feel free to use fractionation as often as you like during the interview. It is a way to go deeper during the pre-talk from the beginning of the session. Also, if a client is describing something artistic during the hypnosis, you can have them open their eyes to draw it, and then when they close their eyes again they go even deeper into their trance.

The Language of The Inner Realms

Our outer, waking awareness is primarily focused on our external everyday life or the surface layers of our consciousness, while our inner ('non-ordinary') states of consciousness are comprised of an intuitive knowing. The inner world, waking or sleeping, communicates in the same language as our dreams. We sometimes have quite bizarre interactions with dream characters that on analysis have symbolic or direct meaning. Since exploring the imagery in our dreams can lead to self-discovery, why not also accept the 'out-of-this-world' imagery arising during a waking inner journey? Allowing these images and their stories to reveal their unconscious purpose and significance can reveal profound meaning and depth; the imaginal communications of the inner realms originate from within our own inner landscape and are part of us. They are a fundamental expression of who we are.

Interdimensional Travel

Through the exploration of self initiated journeys into quantum-oriented realisations we are able to move into various realities that are infinite in spectrum but specific to the individual. We may meet those who have passed on, other life forms, and we can travel backwards or forwards in time, within our own or parallel realities. Our higher consciousness or a higher aspect of ourselves directs and oversees these journeys, but may not show itself visibly while doing so. Entering dimensions has been described as passing through a membrane, diving through a still, watery type fabric, moving through spirals or tunnels, passing through colours and more. People have described feeling pulled, and floating into what we would call wormholes and vortexes. When they are moving through them the clients don't use their own power, as there seems to be a force moving them along. Some describe this motion as fast but pleasant, yet some cannot be rushed, no matter how you may try to move them forward at a faster pace.

Occasionally, when an opening is seen, a client may take a moment to decide if they want to enter it. They could find themselves in a void, experiencing 'nothing', or in a black or opaque space. None of this matters as your response is the same: you will be helping them to integrate their awareness within that space, helping their sensory abilities to perceive and experience the environment, and encouraging some form of movement to discover what happens next.

The SC may have a past life or a story that awaits them when they exit this experience, and they may need encouragement to move forward through this if it is quite emotive or there is a fear of the unknown. In such a case it is good to ask what the client is feeling throughout the experience, while you creatively find a way to help them release the energy charge of discomfort. Remind them that their soul has already survived this, and they are only doing a review at this point, before moving on to the next experience. The client may become silent for a long period of time, as they lay there trying to make sense of something that seems to have no previous reference point. Allow the silence — but ask a few searching questions, providing them with focus. This offers them the opportunity to shift their awareness by choosing what they would like to become more aware of. Moving through dimensions occurs in many different ways and always leads to the unfolding of a story or a meeting of some kind.

Experience has taught me that, when we move through dimensions, we access a multitude of experiences that are alive and active in real time. Moving through dimensions also creates a range of internal realities that always matches where the experiencer finds him or herself in their present life. First they may describe other 'beings' that are there, and then when asked to describe themselves, they notice that they look very similar. This is not surprising as consciousness is formless although it will identify itself in similar ways with whatever form is being experienced.

A session story:
Learning the Value of Life

One morning I received an intriguing message from a potential client, and it read like this:

"I remember always being different when I was little. I was very nervous and timid and didn't like other kids much, as I found them to be too loud and violent. I was always fascinated with technology and started learning to program computers at a young age – really as soon as they became available – and my fascination has continued to this day. I am still nervous, but have learned to deal with emotions to a degree, sensitive, but am also good with people. Now I'm in a profession where I have to deal with them every day and I'm good at it.

At 19 years of age I saw a large UFO at the back of my house. I had no contact but it made a lasting impression on me, which led to a passion for UFOs from that point onwards.

Over the last few years I have had the feeling I'm being visited at night and keep waking up in strange positions – sometimes out of my bed. I don't have any physical signs but have made some recordings of night noises and have heard strange buzzing sounds.

I became obsessed with writing a novel and wrote about aliens, of course, so I started to research the subject and discovered Dolores Cannon, along with some other sources. I have an insatiable desire to know more, and I feel like I have at least found some answers to what is going on. Dolores' work spoke to me of truth.

Also, I recently went to Egypt – I don't know why, I just had to go – and had another UFO experience. Beforehand, I was wondering: 'How long will it be before the world is aware of aliens?' In response, I got a message that kept looping around in my head that said, 'two more years,' although I don't know what that relates to exactly.

In regards to my health, I've had M.E. (Myalgic Encephalomyelitis) for many years, throughout my twenties and thirties, and am still not fully well. I tend to get sick easily and have entire months where I have little energy. I often get a cloudy head and feel like I can't remember much. During the last few years I've had a lot of funny things going on in my heart, it has been racing with anxiety, yet it has been tested and is normal. Recently, it keeps jumping and jolting me, at which point I get a funny headache. From Dolores' work I wonder if my DNA is changing, it certainly feels like it.

I've always been a little depressed all of my life but since I've been exploring concepts around ETs I've become calmer and happier. There's no reason to be depressed, apart from ill health. I have a good job, a nice place to live and a good relationship. But I still feel like ending my life a lot.

Also, I just want to know where I am from and what I'm meant to be doing here."

As I read this client's letter, my first thought was that the session was going to be 'interesting'. When Jerry arrived he was an attractive, clean-cut, successful businessman in his forties. He was also nervous — and wondered if he would be able to go into trance or provide information — but he needn't have been worried...

His special place is a peaceful setting in a valley. Though when he is asked to sit on a cloud his stomach feels very anxious, and he continues to feel tightness in his chest at the thought of it. My own mind begins to question his ability to have a successful session, but those concerns are quickly overridden by my decision to take an alternative route, only as a last resort. So I ask him to breathe the anxiousness down and out through his body. After doing so, he agrees to 'make himself go.'

As he descends from the cloud he begins to sob quietly, saying: "Everything is very dark and has been destroyed — it's just desolate — dark, with lava and clouds, there is no life, not even a blade of grass." I send him back in time to tell me what led up to this scene, but he doesn't understand what happened and just feels profoundly sad. "I see buildings that used to be there a long time ago, bricks and broken glass are all around." He feels a massive sense of loss and tragedy. He is alone. There are no signs of anyone else around. He decides he doesn't want to be there so he begins moving upwards. I then suggest he drifts and floats to a significant moment or event.

I use this suggestion to access appropriate memories that the client's higher self wants them to be aware of, even if it is from a different lifetime. This works like providing an entry to a non-directional leapfrog, as I never know how they will respond. They may find themselves in the same life, or an entirely different time, space or place. I do not tell them what to find, I simply guide them to: "Something appropriate, where there is information that will help them in the best possible way."

Jerry then finds himself as a soldier — a sniper who is hiding in the grass with a few other men. He is a frightened, young Asian man. His thoughts are: 'I don't want to be here, I feel I am doing something wrong'. He then takes a life by shooting a person, and feels a profound sense of guilt. He moves ahead to find that he is now in prison. He is being held accountable for that death, but he had only been: "Following orders. It was all about politics so this is unfair." He makes a decision while in prison — that still affects his life today: he always tries to do the right thing and not to follow 'orders.' He then says, crying deeply, "Its not the first time." I then instruct him to take a deep breath and go back to that first time.

He sees himself as a Roman soldier, who took pride in taking many lives. "All the deaths were brutal and I took the lives of many women and children." He breaks down sobbing, "I'm so sorry for doing this." I wonder if he's going to come out of trance and if so, how should I handle it. I also wonder how to move him forward to the last part of his life as the sniper. He finds himself in prison again but he is happy because he has paid the price for what he had done. He is reading spiritual books and can now see and feel that he is finally at peace. He is then taken to a firing range, blindfolded, and experiences a 'profound fear in my heart.' As he is shot through the heart he thinks: 'I am at peace and I forgive them.'

He decided in that lifetime to never take another life again, as there is too much pain involved. After his transition he looks back on that life and finds himself sitting on a chair with someone asking him: "What lessons did you learn?" He replies that he took life and spent his own life paying for it. He doesn't know who he's talking to, but feels they are not human and there are others there, too. "I'm there to explain myself," he tells me, "Other humans took my life because I didn't want to take any more lives, and they kept me in prison for that."

Then Jerry exclaims out loud, "I passed my test! I didn't pass it for a long time, it was about the value of life." I say: "I wonder if there is anyone there he can ask about the value of life?" He responds, "There is a blue light, it's connected with me and it's a form of energy." The light tells him again that he has learned his lessons. "I've had to learn a lot about history and live the history to learn the lessons. I've had many lifetimes, going way back, beyond what you consider to be history. Some are not on earth and I've seen a lot of death, a lot of sacrifices—of humans and of other creatures—I don't know what they are. I basically had to learn the cycle of life. Everything has its place, every lifetime is a lesson, but I can't remember them all. I've been an observer mainly, but I have taken life. Observing, participating and controlling, I've been many parts of many things and seen many events from different sides. The different roles and perspectives give knowledge."

The blue light wants him to know that he is loved, and he receives a sensation of love in his heart and feels a light fluttering sensation there. The light tells him to, "Just be." I ask the light if his higher self could remove the fear and stigma of being shot in the heart, and it replies that it doesn't need to be repaired as the lesson is over and, "It is now corrected." Jerry had carried this into his current lifetime to remind him of the lessons but was not consciously aware of this. The light wants him to be happy and advises that: "This is his last lesson on Earth if he wants it to be." I ask if the light knows about his history and it replies: "I know everything about him including everything he's ever done." I wonder out loud if it can take him back to his right place, so he can know the truth about himself—such as where he comes from, spends a lot of time, or where his soul resides.

Jerry then finds himself in an unbelievably bright city of crystal that has tall buildings. There are three suns in the sky and he is sitting on a beach with a human appearance. He sees a brown-skinned, healthy, muscular, strong male with greyish-blonde hair, wearing a short robe like a toga with a buckle at the waist. He feels he can fly and does so by moving wherever he wishes. I ask him to absorb all the qualities of this person on the beach into his present physical body, and he exclaims with surprise, "The person on the beach just turned around and said 'Remember who you are,' to me. He has put his hands on my shoulders and is embracing me."

How delightful... Imagine meeting another aspect of yourself and communicating like two separate beings!

As they communicate Jerry says, "I'm me again." He tells Jerry to keep learning. "I'm here on a mission to move humanity forward. My role is to teach about the past... people need to remember what we were; the part of me on the beach could do anything with my mind. We need to remember what mankind was capable of." His higher self tells him, "It's too soon and frightening for some people to know about these abilities, as they are in a deep trance. So teaching about the awakening needs to be done gradually. Those that want to learn will learn, and those that don't want to, won't. On Earth we're stuck, we can't always learn the lessons because we're in a trance and we are controlled. Teaching breaks the trance, but teaching will be difficult because people won't listen. Surround yourself with those that want to learn, and be gentle with those that resist—even if they initially resist, the seed is still planted. "Imagine sandcastles on the beach, the first wave has little impact on the sandcastles, but eventually, with more and more waves coming in the sandcastles no longer exist."

It was decided that he should come to Earth at this time because: "I have a powerful heart, and when it beats it's like sending a wave around the earth, it goes out a long way. I feel everything through my heart and I can make a difference with my heart—it has played a strong part in all my lives." He's also told his heart is his soul, and the pain there (one of his questions) has to do with the many things he's done in the past. His heart has power but it is quite sensitive so he finds that life is hard on planet Earth. He is also told that he needs to unlock more of his heart.

He is then shown a cave that contains large crystals and is given the word 'balance.' The tightness in his chest begins subsiding. He feels much lighter and can breathe more easily. The crystals are now glowing so he can see his higher self more clearly: "He has blue eyes and is old but he doesn't look it." He is told, "I am you," and Jerry begins crying again because he misses him. It is confirmed that this is his higher self and Jerry is given a name for him, which also ends up being Jerry's keyword, to be used to help him go into trance more quickly in future occasions. He also receives a physical sensation that is connected with the presence of his higher self: "Hands on my shoulders."

The reason for his health problems was to keep him quiet and away from other people, because he needed this in order to learn. His having spent that past lifetime in prison served a similar need. Isolation in a jail cell had kept his energy protected in the past. Yet now, in this lifetime, it is time for him to go out and teach others. He is given a glowing purple crystal and told that when he needs strength he is to hold it, and to find one to hold during meditation. He will see his past lives in his meditations and should teach the lessons he has learned from them. He says he doesn't really want to do this, as he finds it hard, but is told to, "Take one step at a time and he will find peace. He has been affected by other peoples' thoughts before and he's not supposed to do that again."

He is told it was his higher self that has been visiting him at night, and that he has always been there when he needed him, especially in times of need, such as during those times he had felt suicidal. The UFOs were just to make him think differently, as were the illnesses. Those life events had to include situations that no-one knew how to solve, in order that he would have to: "Look beyond and keep searching. It's time now to continue exploring: visit with your higher self in your dreams and if you hold a crystal in your hands it will take you to the crystal cave to speak with your higher self." Jerry was told to: "Go out and find a purple crystal and when you hold it in your hands you will know it is the right one."

He was also told that he is not a healer, but rather, an observer. His heart serves to remind him of the pain related to the lessons. He was told that when his higher self comes to him in the night, it's mission is to gather information from him, as he has a unique way of looking at the world. Jerry was also instructed to walk barefoot on the Earth.

Walking barefoot, grounding with the Earth, is a recent trend that has been showing up in many of my clients' sessions. Also, several people have described witnessing and/or experiencing life on devastated planets. This causes me to wonder if this is an archetypal image, or an imprinted event that is serving to remind us not to create a worst-case scenario outcome. Alternatively perhaps these are actual planets that have died. For example, data sent back from Mars by the Curiosity Rover suggests that there was, in fact, a major catastrophic event that destroyed the planet's atmosphere, billions of years ago.

The Importance of the Imagination

"Imagination is a portal through which you can transcend the imposed limitations of this world. All creative persons use this power. With wisdom and will, whatever you can imagine, and continue to imagine, can become real. I tell you, that things which do not exist now in this world will be created for you. Imagination can be materialized. When you develop spiritually, you can materialize your thoughts."
—Paramahansa Yogananda

The first step to guide a client into relaxation is to have them close their eyes. This sends a signal to the body that it is time to go within. Focused, internal attention uses the imagination for 'perceiving', however, this is not the same as creating fantasy, even though the exploration of our own consciousness can seem fantastical and far-removed from our everyday life. Fantasy is self-created, but there are times when the imagery or ideas seem to spontaneously come out of nowhere without any prompting from you. Even with these types of insight, thoughts and impressions derived in hypnosis can seem like fantasy—yet still, why do those specific ideas show up, and how do they relate to underlying themes in the client's current life experience? Remind the client to put aside all analysis, allowing them to become curious while not mentally editing the content that appears.

Quantum sessions are built upon accessing awareness, expanding awareness and integrating awareness. The mind must access information through its broader, non-linear, non-judgmental state, rather than through the limited, finite expressions of the everyday conscious mind perception.

Hypnosis incorporates use of the imagination, and it is with our own imagination that we can help clients by guiding theirs. If we don't engage their imagination the chances are we won't be able to induce them into deep relaxation. It is always advisable to explore any fears or misconceptions the client may have about hypnosis before beginning the session, so that they can relax fully and trust the process. This is actually the conscious mind needing to stay alert, in order to 'protect a fear or a reason' that may cause the client to feel exposed. The client really needs to be able to trust the process by knowing that the information about to be shared comes from different levels of their own consciousness.

As practitioners we facilitate the client to bring about their own healing from the unconscious mind. As facilitators we help them build a conscious bridge between those levels of awareness through the subconscious mind. We hold space for the miraculous to take place. We have the ability to help others gather far more in-depth information and understanding than they presently consciously have, if we utilise the session to the utmost advantage. This does not mean every session will be perfect, but it increases the potential for the desired results, if we have a variety of methods or techniques available in our toolbox. We assist by guiding the client through various layers of their own consciousness to achieve those ends. The analogy of peeling away layers of an onion is very apt here. It is beneficial to learn a number of ways in which we can help the client to achieve remarkable and effective results. If we do not ask the right questions, the information coming forward will not be as complete as it is capable of being. Hypnosis helps the client become more perceptive and sensitive as a way for both information gathering while initiating future life changes.

The imagination can and should be used as one of the tools in our workbox. It allows movement into and through inter-dimensional levels of consciousness, bridging conscious reality with the subconscious history, and is the primary creative resource. Our imagination is the gateway to our true self and our multidimensional soul essence. Using the imagination does not mean a person actually sees clearly-defined images or a flowing movie—it might be that all the senses come together in their own unique way. I prefer to encourage the idea of 'impressions' rather than pictures, and then leave the client enough creative space to allow responses to occur in whatever kind of way they manifest. Everyone can visualise, as it's a natural process when using our memory or constructing our perceptions.

Memories and imagination can be said to originate through similar ways within the mind, and are coloured through our personal filter or unique perception. When it comes to what is defined as a 'past life', it does not matter if it is our imagination creating a subconscious story as an actual event, an analogy or as a metaphor. What is important is that it helps us in a way that is healing or insightful.

When we allow our consciousness to actively use the imagination we automatically engage our non-physical awareness. Imagine, if you will, a switch being flipped on through the power of the imagination, then shifting mind-gears into the realms beyond our physical senses, which can be experienced as dreamlike, with symbolism, metaphor and analogies. Imagery does not mean that a person actually sees pictures, as it might be that all of their senses come together to create some sort of conceptual response. Similarly our emotions use a combination of senses as a way of communicating with us.

Our memories and daydreams surface in a similar way. Somewhere deep within is a language or imagery that we can interact with and learn from, a source that engages us completely and takes us outside of our immediate reality—often into different timelines. The types of imagery we have replaying in our mind's eye can be either positive or negative, with many variations in-between. Hypnosis is a great way to instil positive life-enhancing imagery for our subconscious to act upon and create as a reality. Whatever way we access these inner images is not what is important, as we are all able to recall from our inner world in a variety of ways that are uniquely ours.

Many people think they will not 'see' anything, so they doubt that hypnosis will work for them. However, using the imagination is a useful and powerful way to engage all of the senses to initiate change. This is what we want to take place, as the body will act on those images and turn them into reality. Hypnosis incorporates relaxation and the use of the imagination. The facilitator must also be relaxed and creatively use their own imagination to guide others. Using the creative part of the mind that is familiarly used even when daydreaming makes hypnosis feel natural and enjoyable for the client and practitioner.

When using the imagination we create, without knowing how, imagery even though we may not ordinarily think of ourselves as being visual. The imagination process involves using the natural clairvoyant ability we all have; visualising is part of the imagination that surfaces ideas spontaneously in the minds eye. We imagine what we give our attention to, which is often an unconscious responsive act. When imagination incorporates feelings, the internal movement this creates activates our energy bodies or chakras, which function within their own vibrational fields and dimensions. Our awareness can tap in and utilise these energy bodies as it travels inwards on various streams of consciousness.

Not everyone spontaneously sees images, but

everyone can use their imagination to experience those informational fields and cause impressions to appear. You can test the client's suggestibility for accessing imagery, and let the client see how simple it is to relay images or impressions that come into the mind's eye and, more importantly, show them that they can do it. This dispels any anxiety about whether they are making things up.

They will be surprised and amazed at the ideas their imagination will show them in relation to what is going on below their conscious awareness. The SC has an incredible way of deciphering internal information, and it will provide the perfect visionary or sensory material for the client to experience and learn from. Whatever the client experiences will be entirely unique to that individual. The SC will bring forward information that is relevant and helpful to this present lifetime.

Our existence is an accumulation of our thoughts and beliefs, which form emotionally driven perceptions that have their own stories. I don't follow the teachings of somatic or body-mind dictionaries as an absolute answer, but they can give some insights, however vague a starting point it may be. I personally believe that the reasons are more flexible than any standard guidelines. For this reason I don't recommend pre-suppositions about why a person is ill, as that would limit my thinking and narrow my level of awareness. I prefer to listen carefully and observe the client's verbal and body language. Core issues are deeply buried patterns of an energetic nature, and many link back to ancestral and genetic issues, which can be deeply rooted and often include learned behaviours. These energy patterns have a life of their own, and can gain unconscious strength by either our rejection of them, our disconnection from them, or our ability to suppress that which we fear most. Facing ourselves or looking deeply within takes great courage, as there are often many layers to peel back. Asking thought-provoking questions—rather than telling people what we think—will root out their truest feelings, their deepest hurts and their strongest desires. The SC will then reveal, with immaculate insight, the highest purpose and meaning that the client is able to receive at this time.

Exercising the imagination and directing its point of focus opens up inner dimensions that are not consciously available to us. Rather than describing something that does not come to mind easily, pretending kick-starts the natural daydreaming ability and shifts awareness from the left to the right brain, or from alpha to theta. This moves the client deeper into dreamlike, symbolic language and imagery. As the senses become fully engaged, impressions and perceptions unfold, and the switchover is so smooth that the client doesn't even realise they have become fully engaged in a way they may not have expected.

Many of our fears are formed in our imagination, as well as the antidotes for them. Imagination is more than just daydreaming; it is a tool for communication and interaction with the non-physical realms. In esoteric traditions the astral planes are known as the planes of the imagination, an indication of how entwined imagination, manifestation and creation are. Discovering how a client uses their imagination can be very insightful in showing us how they think about what goes on in their head. As children, we were often scolded for daydreaming by adults, which causes many not to recognise the benefits of using their imagination to their advantage. We often don't trust it or think it is merely used for creating fantasy, but it is much more than that.

Our nightly dreams confirm that our dream life, while taking place, is every bit as real as our physical life. It's easy to struggle with the idea that our imagination must be making up these subconscious revelations, as our conscious mind lacks the expanded imagery and awareness that the subconscious has, so the conscious mind may expect to experience things as though through physical eyes. It is important to remember that unlike our dream world, in which the conscious mind is asleep, a client can view multiple layers, dimensions and aspects of their entire being or higher self.

An Exercise for Expanding your Consciousness

There is an astral law that says, 'Where thought goes, the body follows.' With that in mind we can access any place at any time with our thoughts. Thought originates in the mental realms, but imagination works in the astral. So any 'body' that travels will be the astral body, which is more refined and less dense than the physical body. It is our imagination coupled with emotions that animates the astral body.

Here is an easy technique to send your consciousness out by choice. This is normally something we do spontaneously and call it imagination or daydreaming, but in this case it involves a deliberate decision.

Sit or lay in a relaxed position—it may help to breathe deeply and then incrementally relax the body from the feet up to the top of the head. This withdraws our spiritual essence up and away from the body, or out through our crown. With eyes closed, look up towards the forehead area, which is your 'single eye' or spiritual vision centre between the eyebrows, and then envision it as a blank screen. Place the destination you have chosen on the screen and hold it in place with a relaxed and detached mind-set; no force or deep concentration is necessary, it's more like observing. See what perceptions come to mind and watch the images change. Listen to all your senses, or feel them functioning — such as smell, sound, feeling, visuals and knowing — then move yourself into the scene and explore it. You will begin to notice how it comes to life, and with a bit of practice you will find you can move around inside your 'picture' at will. I find that if I lay a silk scarf over my closed eyes it makes the background screen very dark, which helps to clarify and crystallise the images. This is quite helpful if I am practising moving around the house, as it confirms to me that my eyes cannot see what my vision is showing me, so I must be out of my body.

Maps Into Quantum Realities

There are many different kinds of maps available to uncover what is in our subconscious, and many ways to explore otherwise hidden terrains — such as out-of-body experiences, lucid dreaming, talk therapies, plant medicines and hypnosis. The map into quantum realities is created by your own unconscious mind, without any external stimulus. It involves a journey inward. When exploring the SC, we can gain unlimited access to all that pertains to our own well being. It helps to understand how to use the map and how to manoeuvre within it, without leading or judging the experience. No preconceived location needs to be suggested or forced. Instead, allow the SC to take the lead and reveal whatever information is most pertinent and relevant to what is going on in the conscious mind of the client. The SC will automatically locate whatever needs to be re-balanced, or it will show scenes to impress, suggest or initiate areas in need of change.

During the hypnosis portion of the session the practitioner is like a tour guide, who assists the client in exploring their consciousness. We serve as a journalist who has a casual, accepting curiosity of the unknown. We must develop good communication skills that enable us to match the varied levels of understanding and comfort zones of each client. Staying open and receptive is important, so that we as facilitators do not think we know more than the client's own SC. When we have constrictive viewpoints we lose sight of the larger picture. Consciousness cannot be boxed into any one concept, as we are continually evolving and changing our minds about our personal reality.

The Benefits of Using Hypnosis

Hypnosis does not require dogma or any rigid structure and is a powerful tool for shifting and expanding awareness. The power of the mind can be accessed and harnessed effortlessly by everyone, through intentional focused attention. We can experience different timelines as past, present and future, and all can collapse into our 'now' space-time reality. Hypnosis has evolved into becoming an incredible way to work with the mind. It takes no discipline or spiritual practice, yet it can evolve our spiritual awareness through a direct knowing of ourselves as spiritual beings. Intentionally focused relaxation tunes the mind into many subtle inner frequencies and informational fields of consciousness, which initiates the movement of consciousness away from physical body awareness. There are definite changes that occur within the brain through the autonomic and parasympathetic nervous system when we are hypnotised. Hypnosis allows us to connect with things that reside beneath our everyday reality, such as distant emotions and memories, which are stored through the function of the hippocampus.

Hypnosis can access deeply buried memories within the SC, where fundamental changes can be achieved. Picture waves of broken, discordant feelings are being released from the client's energy field as they communicate their feelings in a linear way through speech. Then the unbalanced energies meld together into harmony by the end of the session, filling the client with a harmonious pattern of peace, pleasure and beauty. Sharing such visual ideas with the client gives them permission to allow a willingness, to effect change, and it presupposes that they will have similar outcomes. Change can also be initiated in other ways, such as through creative visualisation, affirmations or other spiritual practices, but those take disciplined dedication and a longer period of time for lasting effects. Hypnosis is a highly suggestive state of consciousness in which we can reprogramme the conscious mind simply and quickly.

A person can lie under hypnosis. They can communicate from whatever level they feel like allowing. When there is an emotional investment the conscious mind can override the subconscious. If they go really deep into hypnosis and stay there the chances are lessened, but not if the CM stays alert and monitoring in the forefront, rather than retreating as an observer. Steps must always be taken to ensure the veracity of any answers by questioning in a variety of angles or times and coalescing the information to find the truth of it.

A Body of Light, Destroying a Planet and the Power of Thought

Quite a few clients are mentioning planets that have been destroyed. Often contained within their story is an altruistic desire to help the planet survive. Martin didn't fall into this typical category; he was a tall, handsome young man, whose light-filled eyes contradicted his story. He spoke of his very angry, dark thoughts and felt he could kill people with his thoughts alone. Since he was a child he would successfully move objects using his mind. (Russian research calls this PSI energy.)

While in trance he descends from the cloud to see a pyramid-shaped building in a forest, with bright white stairs leading up to it. He looks "like a hobbit" with the body of a caveman, although "that is not who I really am." A white bird flies in front of him and up the stairs, as though he is to follow. Eventually he finds himself in a huge dark room with a small sphere in the centre, which looks like Earth. Through a corridor he discovers another room with bright white 'sunlight' shining down from the roof onto him. There is a big stone, which cracks open to reveal another source of light—a small, sun-like sphere that moves towards him and tells him something he doesn't understand. I suggest to him he can understand what it is, and he pauses as though listening. It tells him that he should know already, and that his purpose in life is to "clean people." We ask for help because he tells me he doesn't understand what this means.

Help arrives as a smiling monk in a brown robe, who explains that the light is part of him and, in order to clean people, he must choose to give light to other people. He's to understand that life is not as he thinks it is, and should be grateful to be alive. The monk is "a friend" and takes him to find further knowledge. He sees himself as a male in a long white robe, sitting in a futuristic setting made of stone and bright light, which contains a hint of yellow. From here the monk takes him to a forest where they find a 'laboratory.' Outside the building of glass and light someone familiar is waiting who tells him he is his guide, and that he comes to this place often when in trouble. Here he receives advice and reassurance, not only in his current life, but also in lives that are not based on Earth. He is told he needs to know love and learn about his "musical nature." With clarification he is told that music flows away from him and floats through him, and he is to send the music that passes through him out into the atmosphere. He is also told that, "Nature gives life, trust your feelings when out in nature, and let them guide you."

To understand this better he is taken inside the building because there are screens detailing what this means. He watches waves of the sea, a fire, and a white angel on a horse as his guide explains the meanings, such as the waves are a means of communication and transporting energy from one place to another. Fire burns the old and creates new life, transforming the old into the new—it was likened to death, in that when we die it is just a movement into the light. The white angel on the horse is love. I used this opportunity to ask the angel if it can take him to where he can connect with love, and he gets taken by horseback to a city in the sky, with buildings like temples made out of music which is light, and it is a place where he goes to learn. The basic principle is that everything is One: light is both music and architecture; as music creates space and architecture fills that space.

The building is inside a bubble, which is mostly bright white light edged with rainbow colours. The angel takes him inside the bubble, which feels and sounds like a heartbeat; and after a lengthy pause he tells me his body has become light. This feels like an expansion in which he knows everything—like an exploding star with a huge amount of light reaching further out from his body. The angel tells him that this light is a part of him and that it's ok he's not totally light, as there is always something more to gain. More circles of light ripple towards him and, as they enter him, they restore parts of him. He now feels more self-love, and is told he needs to be gentle with himself. "I need to observe life, then I will see the only way is to be easier on myself, being close to nature and learning from it...all life is within nature and to connect with myself I need to be in nature.

"I also need to forgive myself for hurting the planet—there was a planet with life and I destroyed it by accident. I was in a position of power and I let it get destroyed...I made a mistake and the guilt is still affecting me—I can't forgive myself." He begins sobbing deeply, so I ask if the angel can allow him to have the highest divine healing. He doesn't want to, as he feels he should have been more careful and deserves this pain. There is a long silence as I suspect he is conflicted and debating with himself. I give him the space to make his choices, then suggest he might like to go back to the time before the planet blew up, to see what other choices were open to him.

Martin revisits a planet in its early stages of development, while being protected by the bubble around him. "It's a planet full of animals like dinosaurs, where people come to research. I'm in charge of this operation and wear a grey and white metallic outfit; I'm alone at this time but there are 100 or so others in a spaceship on another area of the planet. My curiosity leads to my mistake, as I should be in the aircraft, but because I'm not the shield is broken. I am the key to protect the others, and when I return everyone is dead, as the animals could access them. I can't blame them because they did what animals do." He then spoke softly, "But I got angry and killed the animals, I did this by thinking it, I thought it into destruction and destroyed the planet. Then I gave the power away and decided I shouldn't be that powerful. This affects my current life as I am still angry and give my power away."

I send him back to where he began this journey and he watches the screens with his guide, who explains that avoiding power will not help: "Only through having power can I make the corrections. I can get my power back by controlling my mind, my guide says I still have my power but I don't want to use it." His guide then takes him to meet his council, to discuss the planning stages of his current life: "I see a big crowd of many people, and more than 20 seated around a table." He whispers with awe. "Some look human, some are pure light, now I'm seated in the middle of the table, I feel like a small child." He is told he is one of them and I ask if they can show him an image of his true self. He replies: "I am pure light…like the paintings of Jesus with the white halo and I'm looking upwards, I have the power to create things by thought. My purpose is to create things on earth. I have all knowledge, but the physical me has only some of this knowledge, so they help me. At the moment I can't contain all this knowledge and that was not according to plan. The plan was to be born without knowledge at the beginning. I was born OK, but after that I lost almost everything by losing connection with my feelings, as I didn't trust myself."

He lies down in the centre of the table, as they all reach forward placing their hands on him as a conduit for the light, and the healing begins.

CHAPTER 3

THE MIND AND CONSCIOUSNESS

"I happen to believe there is indeed a mysterious transcendental Something infusing objective and subjective reality, whose influence is subtle, profound and full of grace. Nonetheless, it is clear to me and most neuroscientists that most, if not all of our thoughts and feelings, darkest passions, and loftiest dreams, poetry, imagery, chess gambits, baseball statistics, recipes, quilt patterns and earliest memories of snow – and all the other textures and aromas and shades of being alive – require and consist of neurological activity."
— Dr. Rick Hanson

The Conscious Mind (CM)

THIS LIFE IS the most important to our conscious mind, and is the only 'real' one taking place in the here and now. There is a concept in Buddhism called mindfulness, which means to be aware and fully present in each moment. Intentional focused awareness shines a spotlight on areas of our lives, while fully engaging our emotions and senses. When we are daydreaming or using our imagination, we shift our awareness outside of time and space. An example of this could be riding a bus to work each day without being fully conscious of what is going on around us. Aware that we are sitting on the bus we might sometimes zone out, then snap back out of trance in time to discover that we almost missed our bus stop. Our mind drifted because the ride did not require vigilant attention. This departure from the norm also happens when we're engaged in enjoyable things with our attention focused inward.

    The two most popular questions from my clients are: "Who am I and what is my purpose?" What is usually shown is a simple answer: to achieve self-awareness, self-satisfaction and complete self-acceptance. There may be particular issues a client may have to overcome, but the overall aim always has to do with our own acceptance of who we are. All of this is somehow factored into our graph page of self-analogy as previously mentioned where our vibrational 'energy lines' are connected to different streams of information. Our overall life purpose will always be factored into that structure. There are many core beliefs buried within the SC mind, and unless change takes place at the core they cannot become permanent or lasting. This is because in moments of stress or low vibrational feelings we tend to revert to old habits and thinking patterns. Often this leaves us depressed, as we thought we had already dealt with old issues or our weakest areas of discomfort. It is therefore important to explore thoroughly what the underpinnings are of each issue. What purpose were or are those core beliefs serving? How can uncovering and discovering the information help the client's self-discovery process?

Sigmund Freud used the helpful metaphor of an iceberg to describe the conscious and unconscious portions of our mind. Our conscious awareness is only the tip of the iceberg, like the small area that floats above the waterline. The much larger, mountainous portion of our subconscious mind is hidden away from the conscious mind beneath the surface, remaining unseen and therefore unknown. It is not a lower awareness in any sense, but fully functioning, while affecting every aspect of our lives in various ways operating beneath our surface awareness. The reason for our likes, dislikes, fears and passions all have their foundations within these levels of the mind. No matter how we label these deeper, hidden layers of consciousness—the unconscious, subconscious, higher conscious or super-conscious mind—they do contain our soul's total knowledge, which also includes our shadow side.

Everything that has ever happened to us is stored beneath the surface, but is not readily known to our everyday conscious mind. Every one of our likes and dislikes has been recorded there, resides there and can be found there; as well as the antidotes for healing and all that is needed to maintain our well-being and equilibrium. We would become overwhelmed if we had to consciously remember all of that information—which reaches beyond our present life, spanning into additional timelines, such as past, present, future and parallel lives.

A key question to ask clients is: "What would you like to understand most about your life?" The mind can be our best friend or worst enemy, as we all know. An expanded state of consciousness includes every level of our being, so an inner journey combines our reality to include paradoxes, and not just one or the other.

Allowing ourselves opportunities to tap into the many timelines of the infinite or the limitless takes us outside of our usual experience of linear time. When doing things we love—which are usually creative—we can lose track of time. When going outside of time we begin to use our imagination. When performing routine tasks by rote we tend to zone out into an unconscious state, in which we are aware of what we are doing but not consciously performing the task. We also step outside of time when we daydream or dream at night. Whenever we go outside of time, we touch the infinite.

The conscious mind rationalises and categorises, sometimes missing updated information as it grasps for meaning to enable further compartmentalisation, while failing to integrate new understandings outside its comfort zone. When something unusual occurs, the conscious mind runs through its history of experiences, quickly making comparisons with other similarities within its limited information pool, to see if it can identify the best place to file the new data. However, it doesn't know what's going on beneath the surface of our awareness, or what our SC history contains.

The subconscious is connected to the totality of our being, and therefore has far more information than is available to us. To access our inner world we must go beneath the surface of the conscious mind and use our whole brain. Conscious mind activity is primarily driven and determined by the left-brain hemisphere and root chakra. It has and needs limited amounts of information beyond the basic survival needs of our physical body.

The conscious mind acts like an interpreter, needing to process and analyse, to quickly categorise how and where concepts fit into the belief system, which means that new material is often rejected or just filed away. Beliefs, once formed, create mind loops of unconscious habits, which repeatedly reinforce themselves. During hypnosis, to prevent the need to analyse or process new information being experienced, it is crucial that the analytical conscious mind recedes into the background to allow other parts of the mind to intentionally come forward with information that the individual seeks in order to make life changes.

No matter what the conscious mind thinks, it is important that the client is made aware they should save all analysis until after the session has concluded, when all the information has been gathered together. They are to be encouraged to be curious about what will be shown to them, and not edit or block the information. If we are dreaming we just accept it, so it should be no different when we are in the dream world of the subconscious, which can be similarly symbolic. After the session you may also be told a variety of things that had been left unsaid, which can be explored or discussed during the post-talk, for added content value.

Solutions that emerge from the SC are not readily available to the conscious mind, even though they may have unconsciously affected the client. Accessing original memories helps to clear away any unfinished business, or to make sense of what seemed nonsensical. The memories stored within the layers of the SC can seem as unreal as the dreams we have while our bodies are sleeping.

The Subconscious Mind (SC)

The SC is a multilevel, multidimensional source of stored information. It knows the answers to everything and is connected with the individual self and all other sentient life forms. It instinctively and instantly knows where to place the focus during the session, and provides information from various timelines. Whatever is taking place in the SC realm of existence has far more power than anything we can consciously imagine or create through its art of storytelling.

The SC mind does not directly speak to the conscious mind, but communicates indirectly through the body with feelings. Therefore we must incorporate what is taking place within the body to bring about permanent healing. The subconscious mind is connected to what Carl Jung calls the collective consciousness, or what religion or spirituality calls the Akashic records or fields, God, Creator or Source Energy. This is something far greater than we are currently able to comprehend or imagine entirely. This collective consciousness is huge and knows everything about us, such as our purpose, and what we need to know or do to take us to the next level of evolution. It is the totality of everything, which allows our bodies, minds and spirits to survive and thrive.

The therapeutic model I share here helps practitioners to allow answers to emerge from the unconscious mind of their clients, as the boundaries between the different levels dissolve away during consciousness expansion.

I think of the subconscious as the soul's storehouse of historical data, and the unconscious as the reactive results, the energy relay between the duality of the personality, a soul. For example, the soul has a purpose to achieve having set up the particular character filters designed to provide the right influences to help the personality achieve those things. But the personality wants to exercise its own free will choices, which usually don't include anything that is uncomfortable or limited. The unconscious promptings nagging away in the background wants to pull the personality back into its purpose or life lessons which usually are stories that impact emotionally on the body or mind. The SC contains within itself every level of our mind. From low to high, the SC is filled with vibrational fields and frequencies of consciousness that synthesise together, to form the entire collective consciousness of all humanity.

The SC is similar to a computer storage hard drive filled with all of our life files or stories. So it makes sense to learn several techniques that enable us to retrieve that information, rather than being dogmatic with one point of view, or limiting ourselves to the use of one technique to the exclusion of all others. The conscious mind houses temporary files that act like software programs for each lifetime. Those programs can be changed, or evolved through various levels of choices and experiences. Our belief systems are like mind viruses that feed off the host of our body and can deplete and block energy flow. When we wake up to the cause of our discomfort or illness, and take the steps to clear them, we clean the cache of our old files.

The conscious mind and SC can be identified and defined using Jerome Bruner's description:

> "*Analytic thinking characteristically proceeds a step at a time. Steps are explicit and usually can be accurately reported. Such thinking proceeds with relatively full awareness of the information and operations involved. It may involve careful and deductive reasoning, often using mathematics or logic, and an explicit plan of attack. Or it may involve a step-by-step process of induction and experiment.*
>
> *Intuitive thinking characteristically does not advance in careful, well-planned steps. Indeed, it tends to involve maneuvers based seemingly on an implicit perception of the total problem. The thinker arrives at an answer, which may be right or wrong, with little if any awareness of the process by which he reached it.*" (Jerome Bruner, 1960, pp. 57-58)
>
> http://infed.org/mobi/jerome-bruner-and-the-process-of-education/

The Collective Consciousness

Consciousness is evolving as we are remembering our connection to the Oneness and wholeness of All That Is. We are recognising and accepting our multidimensional nature. We are understanding that we are not just physical beings, and that our consciousness exists and functions harmoniously within multiple levels of awareness. Consciousness is not caused by chemical reactions in the brain, as formerly thought. The brain is a part of the physical body and physical world, and it also serves as a receiver of consciousness. Infinite consciousness has its roots in the Akashic fields of the collective mind, but is expressed through many individual filters and finite perspectives. The collective consciousness is one mind expressing itself through many thinkers, and we cannot know the full soul history of anyone. However, the session provides a valuable way for a direct glimpse into the soul stories that are relevant to our individual and immediate needs.

Consciousness is understood through our personal awareness. Therefore, the more direct experiences we have, the more this expands our creative possibilities and potential for growth. As our consciousness expands we increase our connection with our inner world and the infinite amount of wisdom therein. Imagine walking down a street with limited visibility, only being able to see what is directly in front of and around you. Compare this scene to the visibility that is available when you are in an airplane and are able to see a much bigger and broader picture. You can see the vastness of the horizon with all of its intricate interconnections, and things that would otherwise be viewed as isolated events happening within the limited realm of the conscious mind can now be seen for its collective relevance.

Our heavily filtered perceptions occur unconsciously, like software programs running in the background through the hardware of our brain. The various fields of consciousness that express through us are a part of the universal field being processed through our individual filters and perceptions.

Consciousness is not form-based, even though it can be expressed through form in the physical world. As we explore higher dimensions that are beyond form we may perceive the visible light that underpins these forms. For example, as we move into the astral we lose our identification with human form. Also, during sessions, our clients often encounter a being or beings that do not occupy form. It is noteworthy to mention that clients frequently discover they are experiencing this same energy-equivalent as the beings they are sharing the experience with. Should other beings possess some kind of form, the client may discover they are also exhibiting that same form.

Telepathy is used to communicate with our inner (non-physical) realms. Common responses from clients include, "They are telling me..." or "I get the feeling that... " There is no need to determine exactly how this information is received. Telepathy is a natural means of knowing that occurs between varying levels of consciousness. Depending on our software programs or personal filters, we access what is relevant to help us achieve our intended goals. The imagery or impressions received are pertinent whether they are archetypal or otherwise. Regardless of who and what we think we have been, all of our information and life stories can be found stored within the collective consciousness. Engaging with this field depends on our level of personal evolution, making each person's solutions and answers entirely unique, containing their various combinations of personal experience and accrued wisdom.

CHAPTER 4

BRIDGING THE SUBCONSCIOUS AND CONSCIOUS MIND

Intention

THE FOLLOWING QUOTE was made by the SC of a client, and captures the value of building a bridge between the conscious and subconscious mind:

> *"Things take more than intention, they take the right state of consciousness, and consciousness must know that there are no boundaries between anything. All is singular. There is no subject, there is no object, and therefore, truly no healer or healed, only that which is appropriate. In order to know this, unity consciousness must be brought forward into awareness. The bridge is the connection (between the subconscious and conscious mind) and what results naturally from this connection is the consciousness of unity. When someone is in this level of consciousness, they realise it in the most appropriate way. Nothing needs*

to be done actively, as it is simply an exposure to truth, and to true essence."

Intention for specific outcomes can be set before the session and also repeated at various points during it, too. Beforehand, the client can set the intention to communicate with their soul's wisdom and create a bridge of communication within, as it is the client who determines the outcome of the session with a willingness to go deeply into relaxation, and also remaining curious about what will be revealed. Also they should be willing to say whatever comes to mind, no matter how odd or strange the revelations are. If the opportunity arises for healing from higher beings or the higher self, the client can confirm that they want the healing and the outcome they desire. If they wish to pursue a journey of self-discovery, they can set the intention to reconnect with the beings or higher vibrational energy in their everyday lives. To do so, they receive key words, a symbol, tone, colour or some other thing to focus on, which can bring them back into that connection.

We bridge the subconscious and the conscious mind with a higher source of non-judgmental knowledge and wisdom, in order to integrate a whole sense of self. We want to go beyond just seeing our history, we want to experience a direct interaction that is clear, and harmonise through vibrational frequencies within the body-mind-soul matrix, so a well-rounded, balanced personality—free of programming—can develop. Our early personalities were coloured and conditioned by external circumstances. Now we desire to be free to move beyond that, to become our true selves, and love and accept ourselves unconditionally.

Whatever arises that would benefit from further exploration would also benefit from an expansion of consciousness, to enable access to a wider range of insight. At any point the client can be guided to go deeper into any experience during the session, to discover more or to increase the quality of information being revealed. It is also beneficial to clear away any emotional residue by going deeper into emotional content. If the same themes, feelings or situations have been repeated for a client, bridges can be built from one life to another. Creating these allows us to explore numerous lifetimes within each session—rather than spending excessive time gathering mundane details that lead to significant moments in only one life. Simply directing the client to 'go back to another time they felt or experienced the same', can propel them from one lifetime to another. This leapfrogging of events is not only time effective but shows very quickly the underlying themes that continue to play out in the current life.

The Soul and the Ego

> *"My hypnotized patients consistently report seeing their souls in their chest, neck, or head. They describe soul as an immortal energy essence, a part of God, which resides within each of us. It empowers the body, which cannot live without it. At the time of death, the body dies but the soul continues to survive."*
> —Dr. Shakuntala Modi

There are many theories and concepts to describe what we call the soul, yet at no time during the sessions do the non-physical beings we encounter use that word. If we ask these beings who are interacting with the client, "Does the client belong to your soul group?" they sometimes reply with a yes or "We are friends, guides or helpers." When we ask about the soul in general, we find that the word comes from us and not the client. The labels are ours. The soul can be thought of as many individualised fields of inFORMation. Our spiritual essence, which is formless, inhabits form through the mechanism of a soul that is programmed to express, and experience, while gathering or sharing information.

This longing for more personal connection, which will provide us with an understanding of who we are, clarity of our life purpose, increased self knowledge, will enable us to have transformational experiences. Any external searching for answers eventually leads us to look deeply within ourselves, to resolve personal conflicts, to embrace ourselves without self doubts, leading us into more self compassion, and understanding of any emotional conflicts when it comes to understanding consciousness and the self. For the purpose of this book, when I reference the soul I am referencing the total, complete, infinite source of the individual. Also, 'they' (the collective SC communicants) never use the word 'ego' when speaking of the personality, which is always addressed in the first or third person.

Through my work communicating with hundreds of subconscious minds I have learned to think of the ego is that part of us that is an individual soul aspect. Each aspect or 'past life' has its own specific ego personality constructed through the soul's particular need for its human potential and purpose. There are many definitions of the ego, with some eastern esoteric teachings encouraging us to get rid of our ego or suppress it, however for the purpose of this handbook, when I speak of the ego I am referring to the current individual personality of a person.

The Soul — like a Sun

A diagram I use with clients to give them an idea of what the soul is like, uses a picture of the sun with rays shining out from it. Each ray represents an aspect of the soul, and a variety of aspects can inhabit different positions on the same ray, representing a branching out to even more possible dimensions and realities. Through an extended awareness by going inwards towards the centre, we can connect spiritually with those other rays or streams of self-awareness. As they allow themselves to enter deep relaxation through an expansion in consciousness, they tap into the soul's pool of all knowledge. They access the other lifetimes that will feel personal to them, as at some level all of their soul's experience are personal and belongs to all aspects. Some lifetimes more than others are directly influencing aspects of their other lives.

Soul Aspects

Imagine an octopus with its many tentacles all extended outwards, sensing in different directions as it explores the world around it. Each tentacle remains connected to the main body, although each has no awareness of the others. They may come into contact with one another, which is often viewed as a different entity. Then when the tentacles are pulled back into the body, they bring back their individualised conscious awareness, merging into the collective consciousness of the whole body system, and in return are able to access the totality of all other aspects of self. Likewise, we often meet our past life selves during a session, and view them as independent individuals that appear to be completely separate entities. When we expand our consciousness inwards we access other aspects that are relevant to our current energy system. When we point the light of conscious awareness within, we can access and 'live' the experiences of these other aspects in the present moment, which in reality are a part of our collective self.

Soul Loss and Fragmentation

Sometimes emotional pieces of us become compartmentalised, 'lost', split off or stuck in a past life, not realising that it has transitioned through death and needs to be integrated. Soul loss often occurs as an unconscious coping mechanism when we experience fearful feelings deeply burying or compartmentalising them after we have suffered some type of trauma. It is imagined as a fragmentation of the soul's otherwise available energy. This depletion of energy can eventually become the cause of physical, psychic or emotional issues or ailments.

Meeting Aspects of Self

Author and lecturer Bruce Moen describes the soul retrieval of Joshua, a story recounted in his first book, *Voyages Into The Unknown*. Joshua was one of Moen's past lives, although he uses the term 'an aspect of self' as a more accurate label. Joshua died thousands of years ago from an infection caused by a spear wound to his liver, and had been stuck in the spirit world since. After Joshua's retrieval all symptoms of a rare inflammatory disease, sarcoidosis, (a disease with no known cause nor cure) eventually disappeared from Moen's liver in his present lifetime. In this book he also describes what he and Robert Monroe call a 'disc,' which is what or where all soul aspects originate, or are connected to.

Bruce Moen:
http://www.afterlife-knowledge.com/start.html

Inner Communication and Intuition

Humans are constructed to be influenced by other aspects, to rebalance energies or karma, to learn and grow in particular ways, and for a myriad of other reasons. Our existence is an accumulation of our thoughts and beliefs, which form emotionally driven perceptions that have their own stories. This influence plays out in the physical world as an individual ego, but the total self communicates with all aspects, even if they are not aware of each other. This inner communication comes through intuition, synchronicity, dreams, and downloads of knowing and guidance.

Personal Filters are like Software Programs

Imagine that each of us is like a page of graph paper, with each line connecting us to different patterns of vibrational frequencies, which are different fields or streams of information. Our overall life-affirming purpose is factored into that structure. These universal fields of consciousness are expressed through our own unique individual filtering systems, creating stories that hold specific and significant value to the experiencer. Lessons and teachings emanate from our soul and are stored in our subconscious alongside many core beliefs and their unique histories. These frequency lines incorporate information that affects us in the following ways:

The Energetic Cosmic Configuration at Conception and Birth

We are electromagnetic beings, and the planetary positions have a strong influence on who we are. These influences can be measured and determined through the astrological chart.

Family Patterns on Both Parental Sides

We are affected by our entire ancestral lineage—not just our immediate parents and grandparents. Culture, belief systems, ways of thinking, chemical biology and environment come down through the family. Souls choose to incarnate into their families of choice so that they are imprinted through a particular set of learned behaviours that we believe to be genetic dispositions.

The Sacred Arts

The personal astrological chart, numerology and enneagram (a system of spiritual psychology based on an ancient Sufi philosophy of nine personality types) are just three examples of how the science behind them amounts to personal 'software' programs. There are many other systems of measuring and grouping of characteristics and traits that influence the personality.

Archetypal Character Traits

We are a compilation of factors and filters that are

quite specific to whatever kind of reality we have lived. Each incarnation is unique and specific, and, by realising this, we cannot help but begin to depersonalise what we think of as our personality. This encourages us to experience our own true personality, not the constructed one that has been externally influenced by conditioning.

We often think of our family patterns and archetypal energies in somewhat negative terms, but in reality, factored into this is everything we need to succeed, learn and grow. It is one of the reasons we are always being told to just BE. All that we are is already in place, and through just be-ing we will accomplish that. There are always a few primary and secondary archetypal energies at work, and we may fluctuate between them unconsciously. In numerology, the words REACTIVE and CREATIVE use exactly the same letters and contain the same numeric value, yet one carries a lower vibrational frequency than the other. One is dependent on an external event or call to action, while the other is an internal nudge that knows how to create freely. So it is with archetypal energies, in that they are neither positive nor negative.

Those who are caught up in a state of reacting to what has already gone on in their lives, or their soul history, are subjecting themselves to unconscious patterns and beliefs. Once these are uncovered they lose power as they can influence us positively, although experiencing them unconsciously may have been puzzling and painful. The reactive person is dependent on what has gone before, or what they perceive others have done or are doing to them. This projecting of blame without taking self responsibility is oppressive, but the way out of this way of being usually eludes us consciously. The creative person has no need to be responsive to others in order to determine their own sense of self. This polarisation can sometimes knock us out of balance, whereas being proactive, or interactive, keeps us centred and free to make our own choices.

Self Value

Our values are important, as they serve to direct how much we allow ourselves to experience life on this planet. We all want meaningful answers to such questions as... "Who or what am I?:, "What is my purpose, and how can I achieve that?", "How do I know and experience myself as the multidimensional being that I am?", "Do I have a higher self or guides?", "What kind of lives have I had in the past?", "Where do I go from here and where have I been before?"

When our life stories are looked at from the greater vantage point of our higher conscious mind, we become less attached to them, as our personal filters become dismantled. We are able to view them for what they are and not what we believed them to be. Old, ingrained habits and thinking patterns may reappear in moments of stress or low-level moods as our weakest points become triggered. It is human nature to fall back into old, familiar thinking patterns, and when this happens it depletes our energy. When such problems arise, they are opportunities. It's important to thoroughly explore the underlying cause and purpose that the 'problems' served. This kind of exploration can be likened to searching for keys to a cipher. These keys unlock our 'problems' and uncomfortable emotions, transforming them into more workable situations and more relaxed and comfortable feelings. Discovering this information can be enormously helpful, as it opens the door to releasing the original cause, providing deep insight, self-awareness, and authentic, enduring change in the direction of a greater sense of vitality and peace. Having direct knowledge and experience is empowering to the conscious mind, because it provides it with more impetus to create an improved life. Knowing what it's like to become one with our true self and soul essence is a powerful awakening, which moves us beyond our cultural conditioning. The world does not change, but we discover it is us who must and can change, as we deliberately seek inner peace.

Michael Newton researched and documented his findings of what occurs in our 'Life Between Lives' states, in his books; *Journey of Souls and Destiny of Souls*, and their collective values, or purpose. His techniques are not the only way to access these realities as experiencing any past life regression has that potential after the transition of death often, when clients experience their spiritual essence and inner world, these types of interaction are typical for most of them. There seem to be degrees of our soul's (total self's) intentions, desire or needs when exploring consciousness through the human form. It seems we are all programmed to have diverse experiences as groups of consciousness, and meeting with the group can be transformative and life changing in the long run. I don't label what occurs in sessions or try to bracket them according to presupposed beliefs or structures, as it's much easier to be open and go with the flow and see where it leads. Pioneers have paved the way to show the rest of us what is possible, but we must continue to grow and learn, through the opportunities presented to us.

The Collective: Higher Consciousness, Guides and Councils of Light

Everyone has a committee to oversee their soul's planning, guidance and continual evolution. They may be called Councils, Elders, Masters, The Collective or many other names, depending upon the client's religious or spiritual beliefs. This committee often communicates as the SC of the client, perhaps because they have the highest awareness of the person's purpose and history. When communicating with these higher levels of consciousness—which are less dense in vibration—the client may experience visuals in a different way, or experience a 'knowing' in a more defined way, which is beyond their usual understanding. Descriptions include that of pure light, various colours, ethereal sensations and images, a wide range of interesting characters, old or wise-looking beings, and ETs, to name a few. They also may notice a tangible shift in energy, become very hot, colder, feel heavier, slightly dizzy, pressure on their forehead, expansion in their hearts, or a myriad of other physical changes within their body.

Sometimes there is a confilict of desires within the soul group or aspects as this following session story describes.

A session story: Group, Self Mastery and the Evolution of Guides

Some life plans include opposing ways of achieving

an objective—and this is deliberately planned beforehand by a 'group of advisors.' Usually a discussion takes place within the group, and it could be discovered later on to include the client at another level of consciousness. I wonder if these 'opposing forces' are behind some of the struggles we experience in life…

Ryan had a lifelong desire to achieve success, which, as an entertainer, he had tasted briefly. Many of his friends and peers had achieved fame, and he had frequently come very close to mainstream success himself. Under hypnosis he accesses a soldier's life, the character has no family of his own and Ryan feels unhappy about this. Then he is shown glimpses of second similar lifetime. (He asks me later if I noticed how he just skirted over these lifetimes as it made him uncomfortable.)

He drifts away from that second life into the afterlife, where he is asking for a life of peace, saying, "I'm still disturbed by that last life and I want to plan having a family next time." This gives me a cue for more information about his present life plans. Finding himself at a Temple of Learning he is greeted by half a dozen elders, and with recognisable awe in his voice he tells me how much they love him. They send out waves of love to him while, "Laughing, giggling and patting one another, because they love me and they know I'm still learning. I've not to be afraid, I'm always afraid. There's one I want to ask questions of, but he's busy talking with the others discussing a plan about me." I ask if he can listen in and he replies: "They're not sure about the decisions being made for me, one is sure and seems to have one idea, but the other has a different opinion; one wants me to be a success but the other says I need to continue the same lesson about failure. I feel drawn to speak with the 'success' one but the 'failure' guy is really powerful. He tells me that failure is important; because when success comes I'm going to love and appreciate it more, he thinks anything worth having doesn't come easy. I'm shouting at them that I'm tired of failure, but they're not listening and are arguing and discussing me among themselves. One is trying to get my case across and wants me to have success, as he feels I deserve a happier life this time. But I need to see success now as I've had enough of pain, death and war—although it has taught me my strength." He then begins to whisper with disbelief: "I'm a very strong powerful soul, more powerful than I realise, I can go back home now."

The elders go back and forth for quite a while so the client studies them. "They are white robed, bearded and one is hooded, they are wearing gold symbols or medallions signifying their level and knowledge." Two medallions stand out to him and he later draws them for me. He is drawn to the one who fights for his success and says quietly but passionately: "He loves me, he's always loved me, I think he's one of my guardians. The one who wants me to fail is always like that and wants me to learn from the darker side. He's a hard taskmaster, but he's good, not cruel or anything and he's higher than the others, and through him I've found my strength. Oh…I will be him one day, I'm in training and have a lot of his traits; I can be strict with people and I help them to learn more quickly, and it's why I'm a good teacher. Training to be like him is important because I'm a very high soul and this is an evolving process."

There is a long pause and then Ryan exclaims with surprise, "I think I'm one of the council, I forget that when I'm a human here. The ones that were arguing are what I'm moving towards, and the others listening are the same as me, in training. This is not my soul group, it's higher as it is my training group. I don't like it as I don't feel that adequate." This realisation makes him feel sad about his life as they discuss his overall life plans with him. They then proceed to carry out healing, including, "Pulling things out of my mind and replacing them with love." This leads him to feel equal to them, "Now we're just a bunch of friends." They call him by his soul name to reconnect him to his true self.

I ask if more can be revealed about this true self and he whispers, "I seem to have expanded...I'm one of their teachers; I'm their leader...I am the powerful one! Oh my God, I'm even beyond them, they're way below me, I belong to higher others and they're going to incarnate after me. I'm the forerunner, which is a very strange feeling and I don't like it—I'm not used to being that powerful—no wonder they weren't answering some of my questions as I am the one with the answers. Oh my God I'm really high...so powerful I can't believe it...I'm way beyond them and helping. I can see the higher ones above me and I myself am one of them, they run universes and work from the inside (realms). I need to be more like them, I'm not one yet but I am very close, I have to help those I've just been with, I have to help them with their incarnations. What I learn helps the others as I ease the path for them. I'm now with the higher group and they welcome me, they knew I'd make it but I'm not quite there yet, nearly there.

"Learning through failure and lack of success was good for me. I can now show them what the easy way is all about as I've been too hard on them—they need to have an easier phase of life, as do I. I'll leave their group and move on ahead of them...I'm the next to go and the failure character is right behind me—maybe he's still learning failure—but I'm finished. He's the one right behind me and he's learning from me...I can now be freed to have easier lives without restriction. I don't want to go back to my Earth life but I have to understand letting go and learn the lessons over again so that I can release all the pain and failure now. Love is what releases me from it. I'm to learn about emotions, like pride, which can be love or not, as each emotion has a good feeling and a bad feeling. There is no such thing as a bad emotion, I'm to learn these things for myself."

All of the above took place before we spoke in great detail with his higher self. Information was provided to show the significance of being helped by those vibrating above us, and through our own learning we are guided to evolve into becoming them. In turn we help the others coming after us. Ryan now knows he has to make the choices and take the actions for himself—which is perhaps a test of self-mastery.

CHAPTER 5

USING YOUR BRAIN

If WE THINK of the mind—or even the brain—as a computer, our questions are the search words that make the answers spontaneously available without any help or interference from the conscious mind. The subconscious mind (SC) is omnipresent and cannot be boxed into intellectual concepts as to how it works, because it does this in ways that transcend our current ability to understand completely. Throughout these pages I will speak collectively of the SC, so as to represent the totality of the sub or unconscious mind.

The brain in hypnosis is important, as the concepts experienced have to be decoded through the individual's understanding of what is being received, processed, and then communicated back. The client provides a synopsis of what they are experiencing by condensing it down into language. The way a person thinks, lives their life, or the profession that they are most involved with, will colour what gets communicated back to you during the session. A scientifically-minded person may explain things in technical terms, architects and builders may speak more structurally, artists may describe it creatively in ways that make sense to them but may not be obvious to you, homeopaths may give themselves prescriptions, and so on. The use of language is limiting and can produce slight barriers when trying to explain things in English, if that is not the first language. In those cases, allow the client to describe and answer their own questions in their own language, which reduces stress and does not require conscious thought or effort. After all, the information provided on the recording that is being made of the session is ultimately for them to listen to after.

Left or right brained

Research into the brain tells us that both hemispheres can no longer be as clearly defined in function as previously thought. A left-brained person is often seen as primarily the analytical, controlling type; while the right-brained person is thought to be more intuitive and creative. For the purpose of this handbook, whenever I use the term left-brain, it is in reference to a mind that has difficulty relinquishing control of the conscious aspect. By feeling prejudiced about this hemisphere we create fears that can be felt subconsciously by the client, who may then respond with difficulty when trying to relax deeply.

Whether we know in advance or not that a client is 'left-brained', or just simply resistant, won't matter if we take precautions during the initial stages of our pre-talk to avoid any anticipated difficulties. We want to create an environment where we are able to negotiate a contract between the brain hemispheres, so there can be no self-sabotage.

"How is that possible?" you may ask. Well, the answer is quite simple: get the whole person into an agreed-upon goal, by negotiating what is expected of them or both hemispheres, for example the logical and creative mind-body-spirit of the total self.

I perceive the left hemisphere to be aligned with the survival-oriented root chakra, which is primarily concerned with day-to-day life management and is focused on linear experiences that are identified by time. The right hemisphere is where inspired intuitive abilities are stimulated, which encapsulates all other energy centres.

Of course it is not that clear-cut or defined, but for argument's sake, we can use this model to proceed. Any session exploration needs to incorporate the unification of both brain hemispheres. This utilises the whole brain function, which activates our inner vision where dream imagery and archetypal symbolism is stored. Deep within the SC is our personal and collective unconscious language, and universal concepts that are accessible through the use of our imagination.

A left-brained person may discount the imagery they are receiving, as they may have expected information to appear in a different manner. For instance, they may have expected to see streaming imagery like a movie, and not the sporadic, seemingly disconnected images or impressions that might show up. An expectation to experience a continuous story, like reading a book, may also trip them up, and their conscious mind may become too focused on trying to make sense of it all. This prevents them from spontaneously sharing what is occurring for them. You will often seen rapid eye movements (REM) that confirms the brain/mind activity although they remain silently processing.

Sometimes a client's beliefs and expectations will take precedence no matter how skilled you are in eliciting information from them for the recording. I have found left-brained clients tend to receive information in a sequential manner; and many right-brained clients receive it through their feelings or senses. With many left-brained clients, their SC dialogue tends to be shorter, monosyllabic or with fewer words, as compared to right-brained people. It might also be that depending on the personality of the lifetime being described where the soul aspect was primarily left-brained functioning or not, that the information will also present itself in different ways.

During trance states, our brains are still decoding information in line with how our brains are most frequently used consciously, especially when the trance state is lighter. A predominately right-brained person may see images or feel emotions that they then describe in creative disjointed ways, while a person more accustomed to using their left hemisphere may use fewer words and search to locate the right words to express their experience in a more linear way. I often notice that left-brainers tend to cry expressively over emotional things that they experience. For example, they meet their guides or soul family and suddenly burst into tears.

When asked why they are crying they say something along the lines of, "They love me." I suspect that intense feelings of love are overwhelming at a feeling level of the heart, since this is not the usual way that intellectual individuals generally process life.

I've found that the right-brainers usually spend time daydreaming, using their imagination, or they come from family backgrounds where they have developed dissociative behaviours, which preconditioned them to vacate their bodies easily and function outside of time and space.

The left-brainer is considered to be analytic and critical, which of course are traits of the conscious mind. Hypnosis, therefore, is geared to put the left brain at rest, in order to allow communication with the right brain, or levels of consciousness that reside beneath our conscious awareness. To prevent any conflicts between the conscious and subconscious minds, we focus on keeping a 'yes' mind-set. Therefore it is most productive to become soft in approach, and learn how to use effective communication skills.

Brain Wave States

Energy flows through the brain. Four brainwave states have previously been identified and written about—beta, alpha, theta and delta, but a fifth gamma is now coming into recognition as the super-conscious state. These brainwaves are not clearly delineated as they fluctuate as ranges within each state. As an example, we can have a high and low alpha state.

Alpha has many possibilities for change but

preferably we want to achieve a theta state, which lessens the intrusion of the client's conscious mind. It is far more productive to ensure the client has no body awareness, that they are lying comfortably and well supported, to prevent aches or pains from developing and remove conscious body awareness. Also, it's best to suggest that they drop their chin towards their chest, even while lying down. Otherwise they are not able to deeply relax, due to pressure building up at the back of the neck.

Alpha is a mentally altered brain state that grants access to the inner realms, no matter what means we use to achieve that end. The collapsing of external reality, as awareness shifts, slows down bodily functions and brings everything to rest in a suspended state of calm. This frees the mind to drift into an expanded state of awareness. Alpha is also triggered when our brain electricity changes, such as when our bodies prepare for sleep, when we leave our physical concerns behind in the material world. Alpha is also active as we begin awakening from sleep, before shifting back fully into beta. It produces that semi-conscious, dreamy feeling which can spontaneously pop random hallucinations into our awareness. Sleep paralysis can occur during alpha, when we may think we are awake but our consciousness has not yet fully phased back into the body, so we are unable to fully operate it.

Our emotions connect us to theta when we are in trance. The theta brainwave state is internally directed, enabling immediate change, and any heightened emotion will connect us to this brain state as a form of physical dissociation where we lose body awareness. We enter theta when we are involved in emotional disturbances—this produces an unconscious trance state—because when we don't like how we are feeling, or are experiencing memories of past failures, we are often not physically grounded in our bodies, as our body is not always a comfortable place to be. We revisit the original feeling or trance state that was locked or anchored in our energy field whenever we feel low, tired, stressed or emotional. We can use intentional hypnosis to revisit these events whenever we want, to heal and release the blocked energy that is stuck there. Once we understand the causes we can choose different outcomes.

The gateway through the imagination switches the brain into alpha, where we can easily slip into relief from the intensity of the beta state. Therefore, we can immediately access different timelines such as our past, present life, the future, or even parallel events that are occurring elsewhere. Theta can access all of them, and expand out further to include active contact with other vibrational beings as we too, are vibrational beings, our body basically being flesh encasing a matrix of energy patterns. At our core we are electro-magnetic energy, fields entwined with a multitude of 'software programs.'

The alpha and theta brainwave states connect us to altered states of reality in which we directly experience the non-physical. It's not surprising that, during the formative years, children stay primarily in the alpha state, leading them to often speak of other selves or past lives. Some children speak of seeing unseen friends or people that have passed away, even though they would not ordinarily know about such things, people or events. Their consciousness, which is naturally in an expanded state of awareness, is far more imaginative and creative than most adults, who function largely in beta state throughout the day.

Closed eyes, rolled upwards into the forehead is directly connected to the alpha brainwave state, which opens up our creative-self, also known as our imagination. There is no need to ask the client to assume this eye position, but it does help when explaining to them how easily the body and mind work together. Through the use of simple relaxation techniques they can easily attain deep relaxation and altered states of consciousness.

The brain, compared to a computer, also has brainwave patterns that are in sync with cosmic pulses (the Earth's is called the Schumann Resonance). Schumann describes that the Earth itself has a vibrational pulse. When we are in a hurried state, our brains are operating in the beta, or alert state. When we are more relaxed, our brainwaves slow down into alpha and then shifts into theta. When we daydream but are still aware of our body, we are in the alpha state. Theta state occurs when we disconnect from any body awareness and connect to our super-conscious mind. From there we move into the delta state, or somnambulism, where super deep healing can take place. Our goal is to shift our clients from beta (full conscious awareness) to alpha (relaxation and imagination) to theta (no body awareness) and then into delta (somnambulism), if the client and practitioner wish to go this deep.

CHAPTER 6

THE FACILITATOR
Putting Your Heart and Intention into Providing the Foundation for a Successful Journey

The Heart, Emotions and Love Coherence

"*Research has shown that the heart communicates to the brain in four major ways: neurologically (through the transmission of nerve impulses), biochemically (via hormones and neurotransmitters), biophysically (through pressure waves), and energetically (through electromagnetic field interactions)... Communication along all these conduits significantly affects the brain's activity... Coherence is the state when the heart, mind and emotions are in energetic alignment and cooperation.*

"*It is a state that builds resiliency — personal energy is accumulated, not wasted — leaving more energy to manifest intentions and harmonious outcomes.*"

—Dr. Rollin McCraty, Institute of HeartMath
   Research Director

HEART AND BRAIN coherence is an important factor for healing to take place. Our feelings are a combination of thoughts that are often externally manipulated, that then create beliefs which emotionally impact our biology. Or, feelings stem from our thoughts, combined with the emotions that register in the body. The power of belief literally changes matter, determines the quality of our lives, and the state of our health. When there is healing, either physically or through insights or feelings being accessed during the session, then having the client integrate it—by breathing the healing in and accepting it at a deep cellular level—will help them to retain it at a feeling level. When the mind is accepting and the body experiencing, this creates cohesion.

When feelings or emotions are suppressed our subtle bodies store them by creating areas of blocked or condensed energy, causing a loss of vitality. The repressed feelings do not need to be fully identified for healing to occur, as the emotional content will show a theme that is played out in several of the client's stories. Discovering one or two related situations can be insightful, but the overall theme can easily be discussed collectively as they occur, or during the direct conversation with the higher mind aspect discussion.

Our right-brain activity is directly linked to the heart, which means that getting the left-brain out of the way is crucial for healing to occur. This is another good reason to answer any concerns the client may have beforehand, such as: What is hypnosis? How it may be experienced? and other questions that might ignite any critical thinking or analysis. It is important that the client feels the energy of higher frequencies, such as unconditional love as something tangible to help them know the veracity of their self revelations. These heartfelt emotions can have a lasting and memorable effect that they can return to any time they have a need to feel connected to their greater self. Epigenetics confirms that our feelings change our biology; so assisting frequently throughout the session to help the client access any new feelings will initiate continual changes from the inside out. This enables the client to absorb and integrate from a soul level essential character traits and qualities at a much deeper cellular level.

At some point during the pre-talk interview, you could casually ask the client: "In what way would you like to experience more love in your life?" or "What prevents you from fully loving and accepting yourself unconditionally?" Then during hypnosis find the appropriate moment to ask for the physical sensation of love to be felt. You could say: "Allow the feeling of your soul's (their spirit guides, guardian angels, soul group etc.) love to be felt at a deep level, so that you know what true, unconditional love feels like... ask them to increase it so you can have no doubt about this... now allow all of the cells within your body to absorb this love at a very deep level." Something similar can be done with any positive characteristic.

When they experience the feeling of love have them absorb it deeply into their cells, so those cells are resonant and awakened with it. In effect, you incorporate love into the story, because the stories are always about love—whether self-love, denial of love or the absence of love. Cleverly incorporate the feelings of love into their inner-dialogue or adventures, or find other moments or ways for them to experience it.

Perhaps they are somewhere that they discover an animal, an angel, a guide of some sort, or something else. Become creative and tie that into the love experience somehow. Help them to know love, and find a way to have them experience it fully.

You may even notice the healing energies in the session affecting your immediate environment, with some pleasing effects on your own body and psyche. This can sometimes be overwhelming, always uplifting and will help to bring you, the facilitator, into a state of grace and well-being.

Building a Bridge

The first thing I do to prepare as a therapist is to recognise that the client's issues, problems and desires are NOT my own, and that I am merely a bridge between the client and their own solutions. If you pause to think about those implications you may find you need to make some adjustments to your beliefs about empathy and sympathy, so you can be more effective in your practice. Some people take great pride in being an empath, as it somehow identifies them as a caring person. I would argue that a great therapist consciously chooses to stay grounded and detached from the emotional issues presented, otherwise you cannot truly be of service. This does not mean that after the client has left that you do not ponder, contemplate or reflect upon what was said—or its relevance to you and your life, as we are all humans with similarities. The key is not to focus on those similarities during the client's time.

Trust and Confidentiality

A person who is afraid of relinquishing control may have some self-doubts about their ability to relax or become visual. However, the need for change can override those fears if we are able to understand and address this issue early on. With such a person we can test the client's ability to take direction by encouraging them to get comfortable by settling down in their seat, having a cup of tea or a soft drink, removing their shoes or putting their feet up as you settle down for the pre-talk. As the client responds, this confirms to you that they are receptive to your suggestions. As you start building rapport and finding common ground, you will continue inducing them by matching and pacing their energy, which can be as simple as nodding your head in the appropriate places and using eye contact. People need to know you are listening, acknowledging and validating what they are saying. This does not mean that you are in agreement with everything stated. It simply means that you are respecting their point of view, hearing what they have to say, and accepting how they feel.

If your approach and mannerisms are non-threatening and empathetic, levels of trust begin developing. Trust is necessary, or the client will not be able to relax or go into a trance state of expanded awareness. Also, when you are being listened to fully and have the client's full attention, you can put them into trance with the snap of a finger. Remember, trance is only focused attention. From the initial meeting, we not only focus on what is being said, but we also cleverly engage the client's awareness fully with what we ourselves are contributing to the conversation.

Whatever reasons a client may have for requesting a session, it will be based primarily on a need to increase unconditional self-love and self-acceptance. This is the underpinning for all healing or expansion of consciousness. We practitioners have the ability to help others gather far more in-depth information and understanding than they presently have, through the use of our approach if we utilise the session to the utmost advantage. This does not mean every session will be perfect, but it increases the potential available to us to serve clients in the very best way possible. If we do not ask the right questions, the information is not as complete as it is capable of being. Hypnosis helps the client become more perceptive and sensitive as a way for both information gathering while initiating future life changes. We assist by guiding the client through various layers of their own consciousness. The analogy of peeling away layers of an onion is very apt, and it is beneficial to learn a number of ways in which we can help the client to achieve remarkable and effective results.

Helpful Reminders for Yourself and Your Clients

Focus on the process of gathering impressions and not on the impressions themselves. In other words, be present with what the client is saying to you, instead of trying to second-guess what is transpiring. It will all come together for the client and you in the end. Trust the subconscious mind to know what it is revealing and why. It does not sleep, and it has taken in everything that was discussed in the pre-talk, as well as all the events in the client's life.

Assist them to relax the body. They may notice a heaviness or lightness as they sink down into the recliner or wherever they are lying. The sensation of lightness occurs because their consciousness is separating from the body, whilst the heaviness results from the body becoming very relaxed.

Deepen the relaxation by engaging all of their senses as we direct them to locate and experience a favourite or special place. Once they locate such a place, have them use all of their senses to describe it, such as smells, sounds, sensations and colours, etc. By now they are fully engaged within and have achieved a theta state, as they are no longer focused on the body. If you guide them through suggestibility exercises during the pre-talk it shows them how easy it is to relax, and this automatically begins the fractionation process, which helps the induction go smoothly and quickly. Reinforce that your voice will follow them wherever they are, no matter where their awareness drifts. This gives them permission to experience some or all of the embedded commands that were suggested earlier. Having planted those seeds, the client feels receptive to experiencing a variety of internal prompts.

Remind clients of the following:

Suspend all beliefs and disbeliefs about what is occurring—this is an information-gathering journey. It is similar to watching a movie, in which you don't know what the next scene might be, who the characters are, or who will show up next. Stay open and receptive.

Session Preparation

Any repetitive behaviour can becomes a ritual and, by default, all rituals are trance inducing, which means it's important to become aware of how we, as practitioners, prepare ourselves for sessions. What seem like routine habits will eventually become trance inducers as we unconsciously embrace a particular mind-set. Do we shift into our own patterns of insecurity and doubt? Are our thoughts instilling confidence within us, or are we anticipating failure in some way? Are we doing things to ensure that the client has the best experience we can offer? Have we raised the vibration of our workspace by clearing out any stagnant energy that may have been left behind by needy people we have worked with? Are we grounded fully within our bodies, or are we distracted and focused on past failures that we don't want to repeat? Creating a positive foundation, and having an agreeable mind-set and atmosphere prior to each upcoming session will ensure a workspace for high vibrational healing possibilities. Moving into the practitioner role with intent opens us up intuitively, begins the energy interflow with our soul's wisdom, and invites help from our inner team or group.

Conversely, staying in a critical, doubtful mind-set limits our range of reaching higher wisdom, as our subconscious fears will supersede any expectations of authentic success. It is never a good thing to be analysing or judging what people are saying when they are in a suggestible trance state, so be careful not to engage your own negative critical thinking. You don't want yourself or your client to shift into left-brain activity during the session, while having to process your assumptions.

Infinity Tool for Practitioners

Imagine the number 8 turned on its side, so that you and your client are each within your own personal circle although still connected. Then imagine that this 8 is made of pure golden light, which stays energetically flowing in motion. Like the infinity symbol it is timeless, existing outside of time and space, which makes it a multidimensional, high vibrational life supportive energy. It protects the sacred space of both you and your client and raises your vibration because it has the frequency of gold light. Surrounding yourself with this higher frequency of energy prevents emotional attachment to your energy field, energy enmeshment with others, and protects you from absorbing other people's energies.

A mutual respect is created between you and your client, as you do not intrude into one another's fields. The figure 8 can go around your solar plexus areas or you can imagine this light surrounds you both in whatever creative way you choose. The heart connection is one of love and acceptance, while the solar plexus is about feelings. If the practitioner wears silk over their solar plexus it will also prevent emotional energy leakage and other resonant after effects.

Triangle Tool for Practitioners

Imagine a triangle connecting the client's higher self, your higher self and Source above, with this energy in a continual flow between all; inspiring, healing and overseeing the session wherever it needs to go for its greatest success. This way you have opened your own intuitive channels and it allows you to shift into your own right brain creativity. This forms a perfect foundation for healing to ensue. I should add that ALL clients access levels of Source energy, as that is all there is, physically and otherwise. Your aim as the facilitator is to create the best opportunity for the highest levels of consciousness to interact and oversee the session. The non-physical realities are not emotionally tainted, so I would suggest that you do not begin your sessions by compartmentalising the process, or trying to dictate what should transpire. That would involve using your emotional or mental energy bodies, instead of being an open channel for the energies to flow through. Doing so will only keep you stuck in your conscious mind and limit your intuitive responsiveness, which can be very draining and leave you tired and listless afterwards.

Sacred Space

The client is having a session with you because they believe in your ability to hold a sacred, safe space that will help enable them to create change within themselves. Your voice or mannerisms need to be confident, conveying warmth and harmony, and you need to explain things simply to encourage change within another. For a practitioner to have consistently great results they must increase self-love within the client and, more importantly, stimulate that self-love within themselves. Allow yourself to be in a state of openness, as this will allow the energy, light and information fields to communicate with you at a very deep level, going beyond your conscious awareness. People are drawn to you as an energetic match, and they come to you to experience self-acceptance and self-love no matter what their life story lines are. Although they create their own challenges and will have to make their own changes, they come to us with faith and trust that we can assist them to heal. All healing is therefore self-initiated. The space for healing should be one of neutrality, love and unconditional acceptance. Trust in the environment and practitioner is vital to relaxation, and determines the quality of your time spent together. Having said that, a session can be carried out on a desert island and still be successful, as the feelings about the practitioner are more important than the environment, although environment does play a huge part to help the client relax.

The quality of your energy and level of confidence is picked up subconsciously by the client. If something is askew in you, they may not be able to put their finger on what is wrong but will clearly feel ambivalent and unsure about your skills. Such feelings will interfere with their ability to relax completely, so imagine that your heart is open, even if you feel you cannot extend it to any great degree that day because of personal reasons. Imagine your heart energy surrounds the client, so that you embrace them from the heart and not from a mental place of fear, judgment or lack of confidence. Breathe that love into your heart, and from your heart envision it moving out to embrace your client. Frequently ask yourself, "How am I feeling about my love for myself today? Can I invite another person into my heart? If not, then what can I do to make it so?" Use that wonderful imagination of yours and just imagine that your heart is open—completely open—with pure unconditional love.

When you create a space for the highest vibration of love you will draw, like a moth to a flame, many non-physical energies. They come seeking the light, or to contribute to it. There will be high vibrations, but there will be low ones too. When creating your sacred space surround it with a force field of divine love to increase the vibrational quality. There is no need to focus on the idea that there may be any low vibrations intruding on the space, as they might be there to experience the light. There is nothing to fear, as it is just a part and parcel of our source Oneness. If you feel you need to protect yourself then you are presupposing that there is something to fear. If you come from love then there can only be growth and expansion. Why fill your head with fearful thoughts that adversely influence the client and lower the vibrational field you are working in?

The practitioner's fears or beliefs may lead the client inadvertently. What are our personal beliefs about non-physical realities? Do they interfere with or aid in our work? These are questions worthy of consideration and contemplation. Wisdom always encourages us to broaden our knowledge and understanding through researching the experiences of others—as well as having our own direct experiences—and whenever possible to have as many direct experiences as we can, so that we can 'know,' and not believe, think or hope that something is true.

Attachment to Results and the Need to Heal the Client

Whenever we have an emotional resonance with a client's story it can be helpful to explore our feelings, as the client is gifting us with the opportunity for self-healing. Healing, as we know, can spontaneously emerge from mental realisations and eureka moments of self-discovery. All change comes about through a shift in consciousness and understanding—that is why the foundation of the pre-talk conversation is self revealing early on in the session. I find many realisations come into our lives in a co-creative way, as both the client and practitioner can be taken to other levels of awareness through the flow of the session. The other most distinct thing I observe when working with people is the light of their soul shining through their eyes, no matter how their external circumstances look. This is the part of them I focus on and communicate with, from the moment that I meet them until the session ends.

If the ego and emotions of the facilitator become involved during the session then there will be an unconscious need for it to be validated, or acknowledged. This creates an energy entanglement, projection and transference. No longer will the facilitator be a clear channel for the light of awareness and truth to flow through, as the channel will become tainted by the practitioner's beliefs, desires and needs. If we presuppose that we know what is best for another, we limit their potential for self-exploration, self-discovery and self-awareness. We can instead, supply them with supportive material, especially now that there is so much information available on the internet. The knowledge does not have to come from our own beliefs or thoughts

The Facilitator Does Not Do the Healing

The practitioner does not perform healing but acts as a bridge between dimensions, or the conscious and the subconscious mind. The client may have conditioned beliefs like: I cannot heal without medical intervention, healing takes a long time, or I can't control what happens to me and how I feel. After exploring any underlying beliefs that will prevent healing, we can proceed with those fears in mind and find ways to release them from the body. Negative feelings or emotions can be gathered in one area of the body and then released, such as the feet, hands or tailbone.

Whatever reasons a client may have for requesting a session, it is usually based, in the first instance, on a need to increase self-love and self-acceptance. This is the underpinning that enables and supports long term healing or expansion of consciousness as the mind, through its desire to utilise the power of its thoughts, begins an integrative relationship with its spiritual essence.

Healers and Healing

We are in a time of cleansing or rejuvenating our energy fields, as we undergo many levels of re-balancing in sync with what is happening collectively on the planet as many individuals are awakening into self awareness as multidimensional beings. For some, this brings up insecurities, imbalances, or self-doubt, bringing to the surface, inflammation or congested energy blocks. There are many healers who still have the notion that it is they themselves who do the healing and not that they are a conduit of the higher energy fields that work through them. They are sometimes too attached to their abilities, or lack thereof, and so they personalise their interactions with those that come to them. We are all co-creating opportunities to help or heal others that cross our paths, and this can be done in many ways.

We are in the process of discovering newer, fresher, more evolved ways of interacting and communicating with ourselves and others, enabling us all to collectively raise the planetary vibration. We should be free to use whatever modality is needed, as all healing is self-healing and healers merely create the bridge between dimensions for healing to take place. We have all been blessed with many gifts to help ourselves and others.

Our intention to explore and understand our own buried subconscious determines the levels we will access and interact with. However, a skilful facilitator can increase this potential and expand the experience by having an understanding of consciousness and which useful tools to employ. Practitioners do not do the healing. Practitioners facilitate the client in their own healing, through self-discovery. We simply hold the space for the miraculous to occur, and help to build interactive bridges between the client's conscious awareness and their subconscious or unconscious self. Faith has also been shown to move mountains. The placebo effect confirms the amazing power of the mind over the body, and that if we believe that a remedy can 'cure' an illness, then our belief is enough to bring that cure into effect.

However, if the practitioner does not take the steps to cover all eventualities of why a client may not heal from their own belief systems, then that may leave some areas of self-doubts within the client's mind.

It is not up to practitioners to heal clients, but we are in a unique position to help the client create a foundation for healing to take place. The client's own SC knows why the problems and imbalanced energies exist, and sometimes the mind-body-spirit needs to be negotiated with to effect a cure, and release the underlying cause. An example of this is that if the client receives payoffs for being ill, then unless those core issues are acknowledged and addressed, the client will likely regress back into the illness, even after having been cured. We see this with cancer patients who go into remission or are cured, but then re-manifest cancer in another area of the body.

We can ask and confirm that their SC continues making any necessary physical adjustments, or give instructive teaching when their body is asleep at night, when the conscious mind is unable to sabotage the process. When full conscious awareness is absent, the soul is free of the confines of physical limitations. When initiating physical healing we can also raise their vibrational frequencies, check that there are no drainage points from the aura, and prevent energy leakage through negative beliefs or the projected intrusion of the thoughts of others. Drainage points are where doubts fester like open wounds, which are easily affected by external triggers.

To become effective practitioners we must

understand that there are different levels of healing. The spiritual content of the client's past life stories, and why they are incarnate at this time, needs to be explored to discover what the common themes are and how the soul has been responding to them. What beliefs have their emotional feelings been structured around? How compassionate have they been towards other life forms? In what way have their feelings and emotions impacted their physical structure? Has residue been carried over from the past that is affecting their current life? What is their soul group's mission'? What is their individual purpose? How responsibly have they carried out their soul's plan? How well have they resolved related issues? What were the objectives of the soul's lessons, and how well have those aims been met?

Healing will occur when there is a focused, direct intention to be open to receive. When we doubt the process, we disconnect from receiving long-term healing. Healing is an inner energetic force that works outwards into the physical body. When we connect with our multidimensional energy we channel through our own healing light, which benefits not only us but others as well. This self-responsibility is life-changing and bridges dimensions, as the soul begins to have more intuitive interaction with the physical self. Being awake means being aware, present and grounded. For the healing light to have permanent results the vehicle/body becomes a transducer and needs grounding, as with all electrical appliances. We are, after all, electromagnetic beings.

Exercise To Prepare for a Session

This is a beautiful exercise to do prior to a session, to unite our SC with the client's and Source, and raise the vibration to the highest healing potential. The exercise comes from the book, *The Subtle Body Practice Manual: A Comprehensive Guide to Energy Healing* by Cyndi Dale:

"The three steps of spirit-to-spirit:

1. Affirm that you are a full, powerful and loving spiritual being. Breathe into your heart while making this affirmation and feel the resulting shifts in your energetic fields.

2. Affirm that the other person is also a fully developed and loving spiritual being. Sense the presence of his or her personal spirit and engage with this aspect of the other. Feel how the unhealthy connections release and only love remains.

(This step can also be done between you and an entire group of people, such as your family, business community, or between you and an animal.)

3. Call upon the presence of the great or Holy Spirit (SC), which immediately shifts the situation into whatever it is supposed to be, providing any necessary insight, protection, healing or act of grace."

CHAPTER 7

WORKING WITH OTHERS: THE PRE-TALK FOUNDATION

If you cannot explain it simply, you do not understand it well enough. — Albert Einstein

Match the Client's Level of Understanding

USING EINSTEIN'S MAXIM as a starting point, it is helpful to practise thinking of the many ways the same concepts can be explained. To be most effective in this work we have to gauge our level of explanation to suit the understanding of the individual. If we have metaphysically-minded clients, then our terminologies and explanations may be somewhat different to that of those with less 'spiritual' awareness. However, when doing this work we might find those most in need of help in bridging the physical with the spiritual are 'ordinary' people, who have not consciously thought about spiritual healing. Finding common ground with the client, while helping them relax while establishing a 'yes' mind-set involves pacing our speech and vibration with that of the client.

Deep, emotionally suppressed energy can rise to the surface very quickly when relaxing into the session. Sudden bursts of tears can erupt as soon as the client lies down, or when hypnosis starts. I've even experienced a client's major emotional release as soon as I've opened my door to greet them, before the session even started. If and when this happens allow the client time and space to express themselves.

Viewing the Client as Whole

There are many reasons why a soul creates an aspect of itself to come into physical incarnation. Often we perceive those aspects as imperfect, as they come with physical, emotional or spiritual impediments. Granted, the soul does not view them as impediments, but our physical senses do and seek to get rid of them. We are programmed by advertising and the media to aim for an ideal image of 'perfection,' and when we don't match it we feel there must be something wrong or bad about us that needs an external item to correct it.

In truth, our soul does not view us as something wrong or in need of fixing, rather it views us as having the perfect background and material to work with in order to gain understanding, knowledge or wisdom. Therefore, if a practitioner views the client as flawed they are doing them a disservice, as they cannot truly know all of the inner workings of the soul's plan or purpose. Negotiating with the higher mind to fix a problem — without understanding why that problem was created in the first place — will never bring about permanent healing. In some cases permanent healing is not a part of the soul's plan. It may be that, in spite of any perceived impediment, the soul is redressing and rebalancing karma within other levels of its being.

No matter what the client describes as their life story we need to view that person as an integrated whole, and understand that they are experiencing the life that they created at the soul level. A shift in consciousness can happen as quickly as a new thought or realisation. If we are focused on the person as being the problem, not only do we engage with them as such but we also add our own energy to the mix, which can create emotional entanglement. However, if we see that the soul residing within a person is pure light, experiencing something that causes various issues or dis-ease, then we are able to remain in our own pure light and balanced equilibrium.

Sometimes thinking we know the answers in advance blocks our attention to the uniqueness of the client's perspective. We each have an accumulation of thoughts and beliefs, which has created unique perceptions and has been fed with our emotions. Dictionary-style books explaining lists of the relationship between mind and body cannot be the absolute answer to determine the relation of pain in the body of each person, but they may give a vague starting point. The reasons for our ailments are more flexible than these standard guidelines suggest. For this reason I don't recommend presuppositions about why a person is ill, as that would limit my thinking and narrow my level of awareness.

The excessive 'monkey mind chatter' that engages our left-brain, conscious mind likes critical analysis but does not become engaged when we are in full acceptance of the client. By default, this is where the urge to rescue others comes into play. This does not mean that we actually can or should attempt to rescue them, but it does mean that if we feel that someone needs to be fixed, then we are perceiving them as broken or damaged. This is a judgment that weakens our ability to help, because it lowers our own vibratory field and limits the flow of divine healing energy to express in unrestricted ways. When we want to instigate change it needs to be consistent on all levels of our being. The end results are much greater when we don't try to make the client fit into a specific programme. I prefer to listen carefully and observe the client's verbal and body language, and pay attention to what is left unsaid, as cause for further exploration. We can also look at how they access the world through their predominant senses, and can embed using their full awareness in hypnosis, by saying: "It is not necessary to see anything, just share out loud what is being sensed, when asked," while explaining that everyone senses things in their own unique way.

Remind clients that the session will not reveal what is expected, rather what is needed. Also tell them not to expect the answers to come from something outside of them, as the SC is all you at many multidimensional levels, each holding a part to the puzzle. Expectations block the answers and limit self-awareness, which can create internal struggle. Mention how our five senses work and how, with the expanded consciousness of hypnosis, they will find they have more acute sensory capabilities than they had previously believed or used.

Often when working with the terminally ill, we and them are focused on instant cures. Some practitioners are often uncomfortable speaking of death. Imagine if instead we were able to help them add quality to their life now, and find personal comfort in knowing that they can do their best to leave no unfinished business. What peace of mind that will bring them, when they clear up all of their fears or excessive emotions, giving them the courage and self belief that they can heal. I have witnessed some remarkable healings when fear and negative energy is removed from the body.

Expectations

Clients may have beliefs about what inner exploration is supposed to be like. These expectations limit and restrict the process, as they do not allow for what will naturally take place. Even those who are 'psychonauts' (who have experienced many psychedelic visions), or deep meditators (who know how their inner world looks or feels), come with belief systems already in place that can block the process. Such expectations can cause nothing much to occur. It is not that the potential is not there, but that the individual discounts what they perceive, because it does not fit into their idea of how it should be.

The paradox of expectations is that they can be used for positive outcomes. Exploring the reasons behind illness can expose the cause and the triggers. Just discussing these things provides the background for what the SC will address and potentially heal.

> *"You're not supposed to ever be sick. The body is a miraculous machine and it's been created to take care of itself and heal itself if we don't interfere. You make yourself sick; if the mind is powerful enough to make yourself sick, it's also powerful enough to heal you. First we gotta find out why–why did you do this to yourself? What were you trying to tell yourself? Every disease is the body talking to you."* —Dolores Cannon

Thoroughly excavating the client's personal fears, asking what it would mean for them to be healed, or how healing might affect their overall life, are important inquiries to make. Such questions can reveal valuable clues, signs that can lead to deep insight into why the client may not want to be healed completely. The answers may also reveal the root cause of why some people don't heal. Questions that peer into repressed or deeply embedded fears will help to shine some light on any self-doubt that may sabotage the session. You will want to prevent the conscious mind from overriding all old subconscious promptings from their comfort zones when in hypnosis.

Pay Attention to Details

Focusing on the highest potential for the client means we cannot second guess, make assumptions, anticipate what should be, or use generically standard explanations to sum up behavioural or character traits into particular types. We cannot lump people into categories and rationalise how to make things fit. It is easy to lead the client in directions to confirm our beliefs, which may not be valid. It is very important to follow what is going on in the client's mind, and allow their own revelations to surface freely.

People will use particular words to identify their pain, and that pain often involves a person, place or thing that is associated with the story. The story is then held in the body's cellular structure or neurological system, and repeatedly shows up in various lifetimes. In the storyline of a person's existence, pain is like the heading for the content. If we think in terms of storylines and the archetypal energy that each soul is embodied with and by, no matter how unique we think we and our choices are, there will be underlying patterns from the collective that affects us. We can gain a deeper understanding as to the impact on our bodies by recognising that pain is an expression of the physical body, which encapsulates an entire history of personal stories. We now know that for there to be an impact on the physical body, it first had to move through the mental and emotional levels to encapsulate a mind-body-spirit element.

Reading Between the Lines

A wonderful key that will give many insights during the pre-talk is to change expressed nouns to pronouns, then you will really hear what people are saying about how they feel about themselves, or their life situations. For example, change all references of 'them', 'him/he or her/she' to 'I' or 'me' and it shows the projection of what is being seen or felt away from the individual as their unconscious feelings that are not acknowledged.

Those clues during the pre-talk can guide the conversation to deeper issues, if we pay attention and really listen to what is being said, or left unsaid. To be accurate in our perception, we can paraphrase what we believe the client is saying, or simply ask, "Is it accurate to say ____?" and then repeat what you understand to have been said. When we excavate dense blockages it increases the potential for permanent healing.

During the pre-talk, notice the words the client uses, and the type of stories they tell that affect them emotionally. Ask them where they feel or their emotions impact in their physical bodies. To discover what the triggers may be for identified issues, ask when they first noticed the issue or symptom, what was going on with them in their personal life at the time the issue or symptom first started occurring, and how would they have preferred things to unfold instead. There is always a trigger—a starting point that the SC can and will address, restructure or deconstruct. Memories impact the physical body, so ask clients to close their eyes and follow the feeling, to sense where they are holding any unsettled physical or emotional energy. This will give the practitioner an indication as to where energy is stuck or contracted, and the organs in that area that may be affected too. Here, the eye closure fractionation process induces deeper trance states when necessary.

Of those who suffer from abuse or trauma, most find a backtracking method to be quick and effective in releasing and resolving old issues, yet some may be fearful about revisiting their memories. Their higher self is aware of this, and will present the healing in the fastest, most loving approach for each individual.

The idea of uncooperative clients is not only limiting and frustrating to practitioners, but also to the client, who wants change but doesn't know how to achieve it. The reality is that the client may not be uncooperative by choice, but is exhibiting unspoken issues of fear, or lack of trust in oneself, and is projecting that fear or distrust onto the practitioner or the hypnotic process.

Deep releasing of emotions may take the form of intense crying. Hand them a tissue but do not hug or touch them, as any physical contact can stop the process or prevent complete release. Touching can also cause the client to feel like they need to pull themselves together, so as not to make you any more uncomfortable. Or worse, you can anchor in those emotions back into their body. If this occurs simply say, "Isn't it wonderful that all those frozen feelings can now be released in this sacred space?" or something to that effect.

This is a great opportunity to use the metaphor of the different states of water as being liquid, solid and steam, and how unexpressed feelings become dense, which can feel heavy and solid, and that our tears provide a natural release valve for all of that. When this occurs during hypnosis the above still remains true, but there is no need to hand them a tissue during trance, and their tears should be safe to flow uninhibited. Practitioners can't be fully effective if they don't follow the lead of the SC's revelations, or if they divert the client's emotions or topics in order to suit their own personal comfort zones.

Hypnotic Fractionation

When we close our eyes we begin moving into the alpha state, in which we are still consciously engaged with the body but also aware that we are using our inner senses. If you have the client practise eye closure a few times during the pre-talk it begins the fractionation process, which helps the formal induction go smoothly and quickly. Hypnotic fractionation creates a deeper state of trance with each eye closure and opening. You can think of this as going deeper into hypnosis relaxation a fraction at a time.

During the pre-talk ask clients to close their eyes and sense what is going on in their body. With closed eyes we can get a better sense of what we are feeling in the body, so it is effective to have this take place when disclosing very emotional issues. Then have them open their eyes again as you continue the pre-talk. Not only does this give you clues about what to ask for from the healing higher levels of awareness, but it also allows the client to begin to tune into their imaginative abilities, which are similar in creation to experiencing dreamlike imagery. This takes them out of their head and into their body, which brings them back into the trance state that locked in the problem in the first place. Connecting their mind with their body will reconnect them to the original trance state they were in when they first anchored those feelings into place. Interestingly, the identified areas of the body often show up in a past life story. The client who describes stabbing pains in the left shoulder may discover that he was actually speared or shot there in a past life, and any similar feelings he encounters now can re-trigger that pain and increase his frustration.

Sometimes just being tired or rundown can cause these weak spots to be felt as pain.

As an example, if a client were to tell me that they suffer from migraines, I would thoroughly explore how he or she feels about them, for example: When do they occur? And when they do occur, what happens to them on a mental (thinking), emotional (feeling) and physical level? What is their history with this condition in this lifetime? If they go back into childhood or adolescence, ask what kind of memories surrounded those events. This is important for deep healing. It is also the time to discover if the client really wants to change, and what vested interest they may have in not changing. Are there any underlying fears? If this theme has been repeated or travelled through many lifetimes, what is the message within it? Sometimes strong emotions like guilt can hold such things in place and create prolonged self-suffering. Everything has a history, so it's helpful to explore what was going on when the symptoms first began, and what re-triggers them now. Any fear or limitation a client mentions during the pre-talk should be taken seriously and openly discussed, as these are pointers to possible problem areas that may occur later during hypnosis.

The idea of engaging the physical, mental and emotional body sets the stage for the healing that will take place during the session. I have found consistently that whatever gets discussed or thrown out into the atmosphere of the session space is what gets healed, resolved or covered by the SC healing. The subjects expressed during the pre-talk give me great clues into the client's themes, and everything that is brought out verbally in the sacred space of our pre-session is what their own higher mind integrates and heals.

Fractionation is also useful to regain control of the session with those clients that are speaking in an increasingly non-stop way of their issues, you can direct their energies towards the healing process through this eye closure — sense your body technique.

Always have them close their eyes to sense where feelings associated with emotional discomfort are held in their body. I recall one client who had a bad relationship with her mother and felt the discomfort in her upper chest. As it turned out she could never speak up, repressed her anger, her body suffered from M.E. (Myalgic Encephalomyelitis), and later fibromyalgia. During hypnosis she revealed various stories of similar feelings that were trapped in this area of her body and her illness was cured as the stories were exposed and released.

As you can imagine, each story has their own painful heading in the book of their lives, and our lives really are a book that we write with our daily interactive stories.

Pacing and Matching

Pacing and matching creates a foundation of trust, which helps the client move deeper into trance and their own healing process. The main thing to remember is to keep the client in an on-going 'yes' mind-set, which simply means they are in agreement with you and have no resistance. Telling clients what to do can set up resistance, especially with left-brainers, so if you learn to use run-on or circular sentences it confuses the logical thought process allowing you to communicate with their subconscious and the underlying consciousness of everyday behaviour, also thought of as the lower self.

Labels

Clients often categorise themselves according to labels given to them by others. These could be medical labels, social, spiritual, alien, or simply something that a psychic once said. We must put all labels aside in order to be able to effectively guide the session without leading, we are not here to prove or disprove any preconceived notions or beliefs. Exploring what the client feels when they think about these labels will provide insights about what is going on internally. How do they impact their body or their life in general? Suggest that they put those ideas aside for now, as it is best to have their own direct experiences and doing so is the only way they can learn or know their own truth. This is one of the major benefits of having a session.

However, there will be times when the labels include serious mental or physical challenges that may include a diagnosis, which may or may not be accurate. We can only go on what we are told, which may be the individual's own perspective, but not the entire picture. Nevertheless, you should never assume to know what is within anyone's medical files or history. When dealing with serious mental illness, without a medical license or authority to act as a medical or mental health professional, quantum journeys are not recommended.

If you have feelings that you are not drawn to work with someone, then honour that feeling without prejudice. If you do, do so from love and not from fear so that the universe will continue your flow of abundance, and you will not lose out in the long run. If your feelings are fearful, or you want the income from that session, it could be that your intentions and beliefs need further introspection.

The Womb Experience

In some cases, directing the client's awareness back to what was happening at conception can shed more light on the current personality. If, for example, the conception was not a loving time — such as in the case of rape or another kind of fear-filled initiation into life — then the mother's fearful emotions affect the foetus in a deep-seated way. The birth process can further compound any subconscious rejection felt from the mother or both parents. This exploration is a powerful way to quickly discover the core perceptions and unconscious beliefs of the client. Exploring what was going on with the parents while the mother was pregnant reveals any emotional imprint the foetus experienced in the womb. This is one way in which we absorb family patterns, fears and beliefs. It is during this time that the incoming human makes life decisions based on faulty external premises. The foetus cannot separate its own feelings from those of the mother, and the mother's emotional state during the pregnancy was coloured by how she felt about her life and the father-to-be. As an adult we can re-experience this pre-birth time to objectively view things with an expanded awareness. The client can also track back to the time before the soul entered the womb, to explore any relevant information from the spirit realm and earlier life experiences. There is always a connecting theme throughout our lifetimes; when delving deeper to explore the original cause of core feelings about the self, the client will often be taken back into a past life story. Significant questions to ask could include: how did the mother feel about her pregnancy? What was her life and support system like during pregnancy? What decisions was she making about the foetus? What, if any, was the father's involvement? How does the mother feel about the father and his involvement or lack thereof? What kind of impacts does this leave on the foetus? What are the mother's feelings as compared to the client? How do the mother's feelings affect the client at conception, during pregnancy, and at birth? How do they feel about their father? How did he feel about or treat the mother? What were the effects on the foetus? What decisions does the foetus make about the life ahead?

During sessions pregnant women will often dialogue with, or meet the soul of, their incoming child, or a childless woman may be told she will have a child in her future. The soul of the child may share the same soul group, have karmic ties or be an entirely new human coming to Earth for the first time. The unborn child often shares the reason(s) why they are coming to Earth, why they chose these specific parents, what they are going to teach the parents, and the part that they themselves will play in relation to the Earth changes. One lady, who was beyond the usual age for giving birth but wanted to be a mother, was shown that she would be meeting a single father and they would marry in the near future, and as he had two children, these children would be hers, and they were also connected through their soul history

Examples of the Reasons for Illnesses

There are themes that run through a soul's experience. Many clients come for a session because they feel they have a purpose to fulfil in their lives, something they should be doing. Some have no idea what that purpose is...others do, but need further clarification and information. Life experiences are described during hypnosis, showing how they perform similar activities, in other time periods, on other planets or galaxies, and now they are bringing these skills together in this, their current life on Earth. Often it involves working with energy, water, music, the arts, creating community benefits, and many other creative pursuits. Some discover that, in real time, they are living parallel lives or completely separate existences, as scientists or technicians studying life on Earth from a dual habitation.

Rosa is in her 40s and has suffered from migraines since the age of 18. I knew that everything has a history so asked her what was going on in her life at 18 when she had her first migraine. She could think of nothing except taking her exams at school. She also played lots of sports in school so we explored what injuries she had as she also had problems with her feet whenever she was tired. She wanted to study law, like her father who is a lawyer in their country (where it is not culturally accepted that daughters followed their fathers professionally), but who wanted her to do something else, a stance with which she had to comply. One of her questions was whether she should go back to school to study law, something she had wanted to do for years and which had not lessened as time passed. After as much gathering of information as possible with no great insight on the cause in my mind I had her lay down for the beginning of her session.

She arrives into blackness and as she tries to move through it her feet are 'stuck in a watery substance', and she is 'glued down to the ground.' She as a male, had on boots and struggled quite a bit to move her feet but was unable to do so. Finally she managed to 'slide' a foot forward but was still stuck. Since she couldn't lift or move her feet we discovered that they were laced-up boots although she couldn't undo the laces either. After a long struggle, she manages to undo the laces of one boot and eventually, after another long struggle, the other as well. We discover that the trap is an 'animal one' and that she is in the woods. I move her back to find out how she got there and she describes running with a bear. I think to myself that maybe she is running from a bear, but I cannot make any assumptions so I send her backwards in time to before she is running with the bear to see how that came to be. She describes that she had been standing looking at the bear while he was also looking at her, then she surprised me by bursting into tears as she tells me that he is her friend! When I asked how the bear became to be friends with her, she cries very hard and says he is her 'protector'!!

I wonder to myself if the bear is a guide of hers and to discover why he has shown up I ask her to enquire whether he has a message or wants to show her something, which of course he did. He wants to take her somewhere so she climbs on his back and he flies with her for quite a while and they arrive on a hill. (Remember that in the non-physical we have no need to use our physical bodies in the usual ways.) From there he shows her many things and begins by telling her that she will be studying law as she is to help women through the changing of the laws. He also tells her that the migraines occur when she is distracted from her purpose. They began at eighteen when she didn't go to law school, and was distracted from her important purpose to help many women. She is to stay focused on the 'bigger picture', which is changing the laws, and was why she was born into a culture where women are dominated by males.

Sarah came for a session as she suffers from epilepsy and has done so since a teenager. When we track back to what was going on in her life at that time, we discover that her parents' marriage was disintegrating, her mother's health was declining and she was having difficulties in school. Her seizures were a way for the family to come together as they focused on her recovery. In later life when she had relationship problems she escaped into her seizures as a coping mechanism to have her husband focus on her wellbeing rather than their problems.

John's reason for a session was because he had prostate cancer. He accessed a past life where he was castrated and his anger about that became trapped in that area of his body. As a eunuch he lost control of his own life and was made to feel a victim of his body.

A session story:
Curious Scientists, and Some Soul Aspects

There seems to be a current trend of clients meeting various soul aspects of themselves and being directed to integrate the various aspects.

As soon as we began the pre-talk the client burst into tears, explaining that she is always quite emotional but not able to understand why. Included in her list of questions was a full page titled, 'Weird Things.'

No sooner than I had begun the induction, I noticed that her face was straining to hold back some intense emotion or reaction. She said she felt a tension in her heart. I asked her to focus on that feeling and to describe the first things that came to mind. She cried even harder and said, "I feel something is going to burst out of me." Once we addressed that powerful sensation and got her calmed down, I continued the induction.

Her special place was at the bottom of the ocean and she could breathe easily there. She said, "I'm watching myself walk under the ocean. I'm feeling secure. I am a shiny, glowing, white me. It's not my physical body...it looks like me, but it's not my physical body." She noticed a dark ravine but didn't really feel drawn to investigate it. We discussed what her thoughts were and she eventually decided, "I want to climb down." So she floats down gently, feet first. She sees rocks and then the rocks begin to move, pinning her unnaturally to the ravine, blocking her entry. "It's not hurting me, just blocking me," she explained. She managed to move beyond the blockage and then discovered, "a huge city that seems both far away and close by."

She described, "lots of lights... blue lights... everything is blue. No one's here. I can see other bodies around, and it's me again." She noticed a few other bodies around and commented that they were like her. "They are holding my hand, and we're dancing around. There are three of them. They are loving me and smiling... They're hugging me. They love me." She bursts into tears again, and did a lot of deep breathing. They were not able to answer any questions but they took her "flying through space to show her what she needs to know" adding that "we're all laughing and I feel like I'm with friends."

I could not seem to speed up this process. In fact, I have often noticed that when clients are 'space flying' with a group of 'friends' they cannot be rushed, no matter how I might try to speed up time.

The client continued with an element of surprise in her voice. "All of us look like me... in an energy body. I think they are aspects of me." I asked if they represented different aspects of her and she responded, "They say I already know this." I asked her to remind them that she has been a human being for a long time now and, therefore, has forgotten many things. They told her that one of them is "the emotional body", another is "energy", and the third is "stored information." The beings were laughing in a loving way and looking at her playfully as they reminded her of these things and all of this took place as they were flying through space together. I told her that she could allow herself to connect with them as much as she would like to, and to let me know what happened if she did. "They feel soft... but they aren't responding to my questions. They're not speaking to me...just hugging me. They're a part of me."

I wondered if she could find out what all of this meant. Next, she found herself sitting on a chair...falling down, down, down... "I fell onto a soft bed...asleep. They want me out of the way. The others are sitting on chairs next to each other." She associated this scene and the odd sensations that accompanied it with one of the 'weird things' on her list of questions. I asked if we could ask them questions. "They are saying, 'Shhhh…' I'm only supposed to observe. I can see the back of them. I thought they were a part of me but I'm not sure. There are four or five of us. They are sitting around a big ball of yellow light, looking at it. It's moving and fluctuating, and it's radiating. They have their eyes closed, taking it in. It's warm. I'm sitting next to one of them. I'm one of the group. I feel the peaceful warmth of the light on my cheeks. It feels natural, like taking a nap. It's for receiving energy. It's not important for me to know any more right now, but I can come here whenever I need to. I'm connected with this group because I used to have a body like them. They don't really look like me. They look almost scaly and they have big, big teeth."

(Later, during the post-talk, the client mentioned that one of them had smiled at her, showing a wide cartoon-like, Cheshire Cat grin. The smile had made her feel joyful.)

The client continued. "It's hard to tell what their skin looks like with the light shining on it. Beige, greenish, different shades. I am like them so we are all similar." She was surprised by this. "Rough, hard, textured, fine scaled skin, but it's malleable. You can move it. We are different sizes. Some are tall, some short, all thin." I asked questions to gather more information and she whispered, "I think we're suppose to be quiet…They want to talk to me, but it's not the right place."

I asked if she could be taken to the 'right place', and she found herself at a table with, "someone in front of me… hard to tell… I can't see the face… It vaguely shows itself like it's not important. I think it has scales. Oh! I have scales!"

I asked her to stretch her hands out in front of herself to see what they looked like and she described, "scaly and greenish, pinkish, whitish. I have big feet, long sharp nails, similar to the big being in front of me. I can only see his hands on the table. It's a small table for such big hands! His face is hidden from me. He asks me to put my hands on the table, palms up, and he puts his hands on mine…transmitting energy. It doesn't look normal but I feel that what we are doing is normal. He is transmitting images. I can't see what they are now, because I don't want to, but it's for later on and has something to do with survival." I asked in what way, or why. She responded, "I can't know anything now about survival. It's not the right time. It's almost like I can hear some noise…like talking." I have her listen carefully…

"There are two beings talking to each other but I can't hear what they are saying, which is strange because they are right here. They have on long dark, dark blue robes." She realised that she looked similar to them and felt quite surprised about that. "They hide their faces, but I can see their hands and the scales… They are talking and moving their hands." It evolved that they were looking at her, debating and brainstorming, but they wouldn't respond to her even though they were discussing things that had to do with her. "They're getting frustrated with me, as I'm not getting it. They've removed the covers from their heads and they have small white heads…like me. They are telling me that we are a team of four." The client can't understand what they are trying to communicate because they are using their hands and some form of body language in their attempts to explain things to her. She could not understand the messages they were trying to convey, so

I asked for the information to be downloaded into her energy fields and it was agreed they would discuss that.

"They are scientists. We are all scientists and I make experiments with them to improve 'life reactions' to things, to improve life in general. We are all curious and methodical."

I asked the beings to show her images of how her current life is related to them, how it is a part of them. Asking this type of question during interactions with other beings will save time later on. It also helps the client to connect-the-dots much easier when it is done during this deeply relaxed state of mind.

"They do experiments on me. Why? Curiosity. Checking things, checking how things work, like on me now. Not my scaly body, the human one. That's why I need to be human…but they are showing me it's not scary. It was a choice for me. This allows the group to find out what it means to be human." They then conversed about some of the other 'weird things' the client had been curious about. "I think they're a little bit mad (crazy). They don't know how to be really thoughtful with their experiments, like the ones they are doing on me, which is only because they are just curious, but I don't feel scared or any deceit from them. They are very, very creative…but crazy, crazy experiments! They're crazier than I am but they are fun and it's okay. It's important to know this now so I don't feel scared of the weird stuff. They tell me don't worry, it's us, and it's okay."

During our pre-talk, the client had commented about some strange lumps that had shown up on her face recently, so I asked if they could heal those lumps. After looking through some instruments, they tried a few different things and then started using a 'blue light pen', coupled with a focused, projected flow from their own energy bodies. The client received the knowing that 'the lumps are a side-effect of their experiments.' She was shocked later on during the post-talk, when she suddenly discovered that one of the most significant bumps had virtually disappeared. Very little evidence remained to indicate that it had ever been there.

I asked if there was a name they use to identify her. She was then given a name. "Oh, I think that I'm the wisest and the smartest of them all. I'm older... that's why I was chosen to be the human one." Saying those words, she sighed deeply into the realisation and then continued. "Oh boy, I should have stayed. Send someone else so I can keep an eye on stuff! I've had many lives as a human. It was supposed to be a vacation... but they are not really doing what I asked them to do. They are just doing stuff out of curiosity." As the client spoke these words she released deep sighs filled with the essence of patience, just as a parent might do if the situation involved a child they loved dearly. "Time now to bring back some order... I'm really an authoritative figure, and they are smaller than me." Once again, she felt surprised, when she was shown that she was taller than the others. "I've taken back my place," she stated clearly.

Then she returned to discussions about more of the 'weird things' on her list of questions. They laughed and joked around with her. "They're saying that not everything is significant, and not to take things so seriously. They're ready to take my orders now."

This was my cue to speak with her SC. An interesting thing the SC said was that she is from a watery planet, which later caused me to wonder if that is the reason for the 'scaly' skin.

CHAPTER 8

HYPNOTHERAPY: FACILITATING A JOURNEY

FORMAL INDUCTIONS ARE not necessary to attain hypnosis, and hypnosis is not necessary to access information of our soul's experiences. It's debatable whether all hypnosis is self-hypnosis, but what cannot be denied is that the brain naturally experiences states of hypnosis throughout the day. Therefore, the premise that hypnosis is the same as sleeping is a misconception, although while in hypnosis the body may sleep, and may even snore, though the mind remains alert. The same phenomena can occur when having an out-of-body experience (OBE), while our consciousness remains alert and fully aware.

Talk therapies achieve the same result when using creative visualisation, or bridging our emotions to the original cause. Hypnosis not only accesses deeply buried memories within the SC, but also allows us to make changes that the body then responds to as fact.

Maintaining the 'yes' mind-set is still significant at this point, so check periodically to ensure that you are not moving too fast through the induction, and that you are spending enough time to allow an experience to occur within the client. Using a simple format or script helps to guide the mind to follow a pathway into itself. Emotional Bridges are an effective way to quickly enter trance state, by invoking an original feeling. Having a spiritual regression into an emotional past event is most effective when the feelings are contacted and released. Without this release, residual energy, emotions or other stories may still be anchored into the body-mind matrix.

There are a few steps we can take with clients to ensure that they intentionally achieve a natural state of hypnosis. There are rapid inductions that can be used, but no matter what induction we choose the body should be relaxed and the breath slow and regular. The format for the induction, when not using a rapid technique, or a bridge that connects them from an emotional event or state of mind, to an induced trance, should be designed to relax the client and initiate an alpha state, in order to disengage any critical thinking. Then, deepen the experience to fully anchor the client into their inner world by using their inner senses. I particularly love demonstrating Dave Elman's 'Eye Closure Rapid Induction' during the pre-talk, because it's simple and immediately gives the client a sense of what deep relaxation and hypnosis will be.

Whatever technique, script or method is used, remember it is just a self-directed way of using compliance to prepare the mind to shift its focus inwards. When we are able to Match and Pace our clients energetically, then guiding them deeper into the flow of the experience becomes easier, as the conscious mind feels less need to be on guard and relaxes its hold. When using a slower form of induction, it is important to remind clients that they may drift in and out and miss some of your words, which is normal. You don't need them to follow every word, as doing so will engage the conscious mind if they force themselves to pay attention. It may also be that before you have completed the induction they are already having inner visions. By letting them know of these possibilities in advance they will feel confident to begin sharing their information sooner, rather than later.

Trance states are a natural, automatic, internal reaction that happens when we shift our attention inwards.

We can use these natural states to induce trance by:
• Initiating an inner focus.
• Closing the eyes.
• Having the time and space to relax deeply.
• Breathing deeply and rhythmically.
• Having an external voice guide the awareness to help shift from physical to nonphysical

Establishing a 'Yes' Mind-set

Understanding hypnosis and the 'yes' mind-set means simply that we encourage the client to be agreeable and receptive to us, without having anything critical to think about or resist. The more agreeable they are, the more the session will unfold spontaneously. This is one of the reasons we don't argue with clients about their beliefs, or tell them that they are wrong in any way.

We don't want to give them any reason to resent what we are saying or feel that we are judging them. Remember, good therapy is about meeting the client where they are, and is not influenced by our opinions.

As the 'yes' responses progress, the client is becoming induced and shifting into an alpha trance. This is why you don't really need to do a formal relaxation, as depth of trance can be easily achieved for the most receptive. This part of the pre-talk is actually the beginning of the induction. Other markers of hypnosis — such as time distortion and catalepsy, when the client cannot or does not feel like moving — can also be used as natural deepeners. Everything can become a deepener.

Some people may fear their subconscious by having expectations of loss of control, doing stupid things, or not being able to come back. Any issues or fears about trance states need to be addressed prior to a formal induction, by asking how they feel about letting their own higher mind communicate with them during the session, and what, if any, expectations they may have about how the process works. A question of importance is: "What are your personal beliefs, and what do you think you may need in order to be able to move forward in your life with renewed productivity and healing?"

If someone tells you that they cannot be hypnotised, you can respond by saying, "Of course I cannot hypnotise you, no one can, because hypnosis is self-induced. I only help you to relax so that you can take yourself into a slower brainwave state. Hypnosis utilises relaxation, that's all." Now you are in agreement and have initiated a 'yes' mind-set. Also, using embedded commands speaks directly to the subconscious and once again bypasses the conscious mind. By telling the client that you only help them to relax, you also tell the subconscious mind to shift into a slower brainwave state.

When working with clients who are uncertain about their ability to visualise, we can suggest that they close their eyes and focus their inner vision upwards into the centre of their forehead, into what is thought of as the third eye, or ajna chakra, as though they are looking at a screen that shows or relays information in some way. A natural shift into alpha state occurs when the eyes are in this position.

When athletes use focused mind-imagery to accomplish their goals through creative visualisation, the body responds as though carrying out the physical activity that is being visualised. The mind, when coupled with direct intent, can be powerfully transformative. Our questions should initiate a wide range of unconscious thoughts. Even as the client tries to focus on what is being said to them, they can drift away or become lost in their own inner processing of what they are seeing or sensing.

Hypnosis Utilises Relaxation

The first step to guide a client into relaxation is to have them close their eyes; this sends a signal to the body that it is time to go within. Focused internal attention uses the imagination for 'perceiving', however, this is not the same as creating fantasy, even though the exploration of our own consciousness can seem fantastical and far-removed from our everyday life. Fantasy is self-created, but there are times when the imagery or ideas seem to spontaneously come out of nowhere without any prompting from you. Even with these types of insight, thoughts and impressions derived in hypnosis can seem like fantasy—yet still why do those specific ideas show up, and how do they relate to underlying themes in the client's current life experience? Remind the client to put aside all analysis, allowing them to become curious while not mentally editing the content that appears. Quantum sessions are built upon accessing awareness, expanding awareness and integrating awareness. The mind must access information through its broader, nonlinear, non-judgmental state, rather than through the limited, finite expressions of the everyday conscious mind perception.

It's important that the client's chin falls towards the chest to ensure they are not holding tension in their neck, which may cause cramping or prevent deep relaxation. Make sure the client is comfortable, with the body well supported to prevent any aches or numbness. Restriction of blood flow can occur if they are sitting or lying in an awkward position. Hypnosis utilises relaxation. It is most productive to ensure that the client achieves theta state, in which they have no body awareness. Stabilising an alpha state will lead them easily into theta, where immediate changes are more likely to occur. Trance states fluctuate in depth and there will be times where there is more conscious awareness to the immediate surroundings, perhaps hearing the sound of a dog barking in the distance, and at other times not remembering some of the details after the session. The more relaxed and internally focused the better the chances are for gathering significant non-physical information. Embed commands by reminding the client how good it feels to relax deeply as in doing so their own self healing forces will be switched on.

The SC has heard and recorded everything said, and will act on it if they are relaxed. The key is to keep deepening the relaxation by spacing your directions and having them take deep relaxing breaths, exhaling slowly. You will see the body breathing in deeply which indicates that the client is aware of what you are saying. Remind them that the sound of your voice and their exhalations will deepen their state of relaxation, their metabolism and heartbeat will slow, and their muscles relax, as the body begins to feel lighter or even heavier. Their blood pressure will decrease and they'll feel free to drift, and the sound of your voice will follow them wherever they are. When asked to speak they can talk in a normal voice, and the sound of their voice also deepens their relaxation.

Somnambulism in Hypnosis

Somnambulism is a very deep level of trance. It is generally associated with sleepwalking when the CM has no awareness yet still the body functions and takes action as normal. An example of this is when we are sleeping at night, get up to go to the bathroom, stop in the kitchen and grab a fruit or something to eat and go back to bed. In the morning we find it half eaten in the bed but have no recollection of this. Or we get hot in the night and remove our pyjamas only to wonder in the morning how they came to be at the bottom of the bed; once again there is no conscious memory of taking them off.

Somnambulism bypasses the mind's critical factor or

any conscious mind interference, creating amnesia and time distortion after the session has ended. In such cases there will be no conscious memory of what transpired during the session or the amount of time that passed.

Reviewing or reliving deeply-held emotions could shift a client into the somnambulistic state, as they literally become the character they are witnessing in first person status. This means that they become so deeply engrossed in the character they are experiencing that they may communicate back to you in that subject's language, age, body condition and gender. Should the client start speaking a foreign language during the session, you can gently request that they speak to you in English or your own language, so you will be able to understand what they are saying. The brain is naturally equipped to make this conversion.

The very deepest trance elicits a catatonic state. This may be good for anaesthesia, but makes responding to anything external such as your questioning difficult, as clients will have to pull themselves out of a profound depth to communicate. This depth of trance is not necessary to achieve a successful session or even to communicate with the SC.

Embedding Commands

The word 'command' sounds very directive and possibly intrusive, but is a term used in hypnotherapy language to communicate a specific guidance that will be accepted to ['accepted by' or 'acceptable to'] the mind. Think of Embedded Commands as road signs, as pointers to navigate the route towards self-discovery in order to find the answers that are needed. Embedded Commands are a means of inserting a subtle direction by hiding them within normal language. They are used to bypass the conscious mind and place ideas directly into the subconscious. This must be done with discretion, ethics, and a strong awareness of why you are using them. They can be used to build confidence and encourage further expansion of consciousness.

Protection

The idea of protection for the session is one that enables the client to feel secure and can be built into the script without causing fear of the unknown. The soul is empirically often referenced as a brilliant golden-white pulsing or vibrating light. White light is thought to be a protective force, since white encompasses the other colours at a higher vibrational frequency, using either of these colours or any combination of them forms a surrounding, protective shield for the client. Connecting to these colours or energies is thought to send out a light signal to their higher dimensional beings, thereby getting their attention and help. They are never far from the client, and they do respond willingly to aid in the session. Even when they don't interact directly, the client often senses their presence in the background.

The Induction

The purpose of the induction is to redirect the client's attention away from all external distractions and focus inwards, into an internal, non-physical state. Closing the eyes signals a shift from conscious mind to SC awareness. The shift in conscious awareness begins with a few deepening suggestions, which serve to jump-start the process of extending consciousness.

The time leading up to the actual induction, as you are setting up your recorder, is perfect for them to have a private conversation with their soul, God, Source, guardian angels, guides or whoever they communicate with (as an inner resource), in order for them to set their intention. Doing this, by default, indicates that they are agreeing that not only do they have access to higher wisdom, but also that they are engaging with that help and higher levels of consciousness. They are now presupposing that they will have help, and that they won't have to come up with the information because they're not alone, and are being assisted by higher power. I ask them to do the soul communication before the formal induction, as a signal to their unconscious mind that they are to shift away from the pre-talk and into the SC realm. This short amount of private time allows the client to close one door before entering another. Preferably begin the formal induction before the client reopens their eyes, but even if the client were to open their eyes, the fractionation process is still activating. The client's communion may last as long as it takes for me to give them my full spoken attention. In my view the induction started as soon as we met, as I began making the client comfortable in my presence through finding common ground and stabilising the 'yes' mind-set.

They always close their eyes to have this soul communion, thus increasing the fractionation process as they move smoothly further into high alpha, then into theta brainwave state as they disconnect from all body awareness. Shifting from the left-brain to the unification of the right and left hemispheres begins the process of unified consciousness, which enables the client to more fully experience things through their non-physical senses. This is accomplished through focus, intention and trance-inducing guidance stimulated by the practitioner's words, or script. The end of the pre-talk, which helps to remove any possible resistance or need to be in control, should initiate the alpha state.

The client may even arrive in a past life as they close their eyes before you begin the induction, or before you have guided them into one. This may happen if they have been softened up and relaxed during the pre-talk, which establishes an alpha state, as alpha transitions seamlessly into theta. If you periodically have them share with you what they are experiencing, then it's an easy matter of diverting from your script, becoming present with the client and, no matter where they are, fully integrating them into their experience.

Using an Induction Script

Scripts should only ever be used as basic guidelines to allow the mind itself to create its own transformational experience from an outer to an inner focus. Bringing its attention inward will entrain the brain and harmonise both hemispheres to utilise the whole brain function. Quantum and Healing, coupled with a dogmatic script, is an oxymoron. Trying to narrow the client's experience into one single format only limits the range of potential that is otherwise available. We cannot define or confine consciousness, nor can we box other people into particular beliefs or specific techniques.

Creating an Induction Script

The process of creating your own basic induction script is very simple, and you can be creative by remaining flexible with each person.

1) Initiate relaxation (unless you're using the client's intense emotion as a bridge into trance). A successful pre-talk is one in which you have set the client up to succeed, and have already established an alpha state.

2) Deepen the client's focus inwards by engaging all of their senses. Remember, this is the purpose of a 'special place.' Using sensory exploration of their impressions will shift them into using their inner senses (as opposed to physical). For example, seeing with physical eyes shifts to inner vision or clairvoyance, and hearing becomes clairaudience or telepathic in nature.

3) Guide the client into an experience in order to explore the purpose of the session. Remind them that in this magical place everything is possible. Incorporate something connected to wherever they are, as a means of transportation to another time and place. In other words, as you instruct them to take an action, make sure it is something that makes sense. For example, stairs must lead up or down, doorways open, paths lead somewhere. By now the client should be deeply engaged with their inner impressions and falling deeper into the trance state. Guide the client to experience spontaneous information from their subconscious through helping

them to create further movement to unfold their 'stories.' Instruct them that as they breathe in deeply, and exhale slowly, they will instantly know the answers or move onto something else. Using numbers can also work well for deepening or knowing. For example: "At the count of three you will know ____."

4) Now follow through with the session, just as a curious but caring journalist would, by asking questions and dialoguing naturally about anything that is relevant to the topic at hand.

A flexible script that allows for individual adaption follows, and as you read feel free to allow your own imagination to make any changes that may suit your own personality more effectively. This will give you an idea of how you can become creative with a basic theme, and more importantly that just as you would have responded 'better' to some changes, so might others, based on their personality or way of accessing their inner world.

In the following script I have highlighted only a few words at the beginning to give you an idea of how to use emphasis to embed the desired outcomes that you want the client to act on. I have only brought your attention to a few of the possibilities, so that you can develop your own natural flow and emphasis, while learning the flexibility of tailoring your communication to the individual.

The Script

In your own time, take a nice deep breath and as you exhale slowly allow your eyes to close as a signal to your body that you are going to go within.

Then imagine somewhere above you a big pulsing golden white radiating ball of light that looks similar to the sun, and just like how children draw the picture of a sun, imagine that it has rays shining out all around it. Now imagine that those rays of golden white light are shining down on you, and as they shine down on you they begin to warm your body just like the sun does, and every cell in your body begins to open up to receive this light and begins to feel lighter and lighter as they expand…as the light begins spiraling in and around all of your organs… flowing through your bloodstream… through every molecule and atom of your body… moving inside and outside of your body so that you are completely filled and surrounded by golden light. Now imagine breathing in the golden white light of your soul as it anchors in its pure unconditional love and light into you as it bridges the dimensions of the totality of your being… supported… filled with your soul's wisdom and love for you. Spend a few moments enjoying how good it feels to know that you are deeply connected and loved by your soul and all its aspects, whose qualities are now uniting with you as you allow yourself to relax into this deep and special relaxation. Your subconscious knows why you are here for this session and what is needed to enable you to have and experience the truth of who you are and the wisdom of your soul's collective knowledge.

All that is required of you is to allow yourself to become curious and say out loud when asked the first impressions that come to mind, even if they don't make immediate sense. Your own self-healing forces are now enhanced as your breathing slows down restoring you back to your divine blueprint of wellbeing. Any sounds you hear inside or outside the room allows you to go deeper into your relaxation as you realise they are natural sounds, the sound of my voice even the sound of your own will deepen your relaxation.

Can you imagine a beautiful sacred place that makes you feel peaceful and safe? (Give them enough time for an experience of this to occur and then have them affirm this.) Excellent...Tell me about it.

Take another nice deep breath and allow your consciousness to be fully integrated there (mention what this place is) as you exhale... and let yourself absorb and enjoy your feelings of wellbeing... as you are doing so, tell me what else you become aware of or any impressions that come to mind... as you breathe in that beauty and peace. Now send out the thought so that they will also be receptive to your presence so that you can enjoy them even more... let every cell in your body be at one with those feelings... as you absorb all of those qualities... whatever they are, they are now yours...

Can you hear any sounds there at all? Tell me about them... letting yourself enjoy those feelings as you allow every cell in your being to absorb all of those sounds. Remember that sounds are vibrational frequencies... and knowing this you can allow them to do whatever they can to help you. Maybe those sounds and frequencies will heal you in some way, or maybe they'll give to you in other ways that will enhance your relaxation even more... allowing you to go deeper into your state of wellbeing... as you allow yourself to be at one with these feelings, totally receptive... enjoying how good it feels to have nothing to do but receive even more...

As that's taking place, are you aware of any colours?

Repeat the above steps of:

a. Breathing in the colour(s),

b. Stating that they are vibrational frequencies,

c. This will enhance their relaxation, be healing, and enhance their wellbeing,

d. Being at one with it all.

Tell me how it feels to be connected with those colours and sound? Send out the thought to have those feelings increased, letting them become even more relaxing. (Include and repeat back to them what they've said about their feelings.)

As you allow more of those feelings to permeate every cell of your being there is a shift taking place deeply within you as your cells become lighter. Even as your body may feel heavier and heavier... transforming from the inside out in whatever way necessary so that you are becoming totally relaxed... both mentally and physically... with nothing to think about... you are becoming calmer... more peaceful... free of all body awareness... allowing your spiritual essence to float away from the body, it is now free from the body, leaving the body where it is (in their special place that you can identify, e.g. in nature). Your spiritual essence is now free to drift away, free of the confines of the physical body, no longer encased within the flesh... free to drift and float away to another time or place where your subconscious, your soul, knows is important for you to explore, a place of deep insight and wisdom that you are ready to know more about, that will help you know to achieve your purpose for being... allow that spiritual essence that is you to take you there as you drift backwards, forwards or whatever direction you like…just drifting away... drifting away... and at the count of 3 you will have arrived at another time, space or place...

1. drifting and floating…,
2. shifting in whatever direction necessary…
3. you have arrived in another time or space or place.

Taking a deep breath and as you exhale tell me the first things that come to mind, the very first impressions that come to mind.

(After they share this with you then once again have them fully integrate their consciousness there and into the body if they find themselves in one, and begin your exploration.)

Reintegrating at the Conclusion of the Session

(Reintegrating and ending the session includes them returning to their spiritual essence back to their special sacred space as you incorporate some ego strengthening.)

In your own time I'd like you to return your spiritual essence back to your sacred space to fully integrate back into your body allowing you to become grounded and very comfortable within your own skin as once again you reconnect with all of those special qualities held within this special place...a place that you can return to any time you choose. While the full consciousness of ----- (use their name)---is being recalibrated back into his/her physical body, it gathers together all of the wisdom, insights, and experiences that you have just had so that your self-esteem, confidence, and all of your special qualities and abilities naturally develop day by day.

In a few moments I'm going to count you up from one to five. At the count of five you will be consciously back into your body, feeling alert but relaxed, fully present and grounded, full of energy, and feeling better than ever before having had a wonderful experience, knowing that you can return or revisit those places again anytime you desire.

1... 2 coming back into full conscious awareness... 3... becoming aware of your body... 4... now aware of your surroundings... 5 eyes open, feeling better than ever...

Eye Closure or Not

The deeper we allow ourselves to relax, the easier it

becomes to shift into a pleasant state of spiritual exploration through hypnosis. Hypnosis offers a heightened, intensified way of perceiving things as they are or were—not as we believe or believed them to have been. Eye closure is not required or mandatory for hypnosis to be effective, although it is one of the simplest methods used for inducing trance.

Closing the eyes shifts our awareness into using all our other senses, as there are no external distractions, allowing the mind to shift and centre more easily and become focused within. This increases our ability to become receptive to our feelings and not depend on our vision and its interpretation through our thoughts. This receptivity shifts our perspective instantly and, as we journey inwards, we discover that our thoughts, feelings and ideas often reveal themselves as imagery or spontaneous realisations.

Hypnosis bypasses the critical mind. However, a true somnambulist does not have conscious mind intrusion, which does sometimes occur—usually when the information is so extraordinary that the client feels it is made up, when the CM is alert and actively monitoring in the background. However when the client speaks from a personalised experiential perspective, and identifies with the role or character being described, it is an obvious sign that they are fully engaged and in-character. This deep state can be encouraged by simply suggesting that the client integrate their consciousness with that of the character, fully integrate with the body or in the scene, as they describe the details or impressions they are experiencing.

The first step to easily guide a client into relaxation is to have them close their eyes, this sends a signal to the body that it is time to go within. Focused internal attention uses the imagination for 'perceiving', however, this is not the same as creating fantasy, even though the exploration of our own consciousness can seem fantastical and far-removed from our everyday life. Fantasy is self-created, but there are times when the imagery or ideas seem to spontaneously come out of nowhere without any prompting from you. Even with these types of insight, thoughts and impressions derived in hypnosis can seem like fantasy — yet still why do those specific ideas show up, and how do they relate to underlying themes in the client's current life experience? Remind the client to put aside all analysis, allowing them to become curious while not mentally editing the content that appears. Quantum sessions are built upon accessing awareness, expanding awareness and integrating awareness. The mind must access information through its broader, nonlinear, non-judgmental state, rather than through the limited, finite expressions of the everyday conscious mind perception.

Hypnosis incorporates use of the imagination, and it is with our own imagination that we can help clients by guiding their's. If we don't engage their imagination the chances are we won't be able to induce them into deep relaxation. It is always advisable to explore any fears or misconceptions the client may have about hypnosis before beginning the session, so that they can relax fully and trust the process. This is actually the conscious mind needing to stay alert, in order to protect a fear or a reason, that may cause the client to feel exposed. The client needs to really be able to trust the process by knowing that the information about to be shared comes from different levels of their own consciousness.

As practitioners we facilitate the client to bring about their own healing from the unconscious mind. As facilitators we help them build a conscious bridge between those levels of awareness through the subconscious mind. We hold space for the miraculous to take place.

The imagination can and should be used as one of the tools in our work box. It allows movement into and through inter-dimensional levels of consciousness, bridging conscious reality with the subconscious history, and is the primary creative resource. Our imagination is the gateway to our true self and our multidimensional soul essence. Using the imagination does not mean a person actually sees clearly-defined images or a flowing movie—it might be that all the senses come together in their own unique way. I prefer to encourage the idea of 'impressions' rather than pictures, and then leave the client enough creative space to allow responses to occur in whatever kind of way they manifest. Everyone can visualise, as it's a natural process when using our memory or constructing our perceptions.

Memories and imagination can be said to originate through similar ways within the mind, and are coloured through our personal filter or unique perception. When it comes to what is defined as a 'past life', it does not matter if it is our imagination creating a subconscious story as an actual event, an analogy or as a metaphor. What is important is that it helps us in a way that is healing or insightful.

When we allow our consciousness to actively use the imagination we automatically engage our non-physical awareness. Imagine, if you will, a switch being flipped on through the power of the imagination, then shifting mind-gears into the realms beyond our physical senses, which can be experienced as dreamlike, with symbolism, metaphor and analogies. Imagery does not mean that a person actually sees pictures, as it might be that all of their senses come together to create some sort of conceptual response. Similarly our emotions use a combination of senses as a way of communicating with us.

Our memories and daydreams surface in a similar way. Somewhere deep within is a language or imagery that we can interact with and learn from, a source that engages us completely and takes us outside of our immediate reality — often into different timelines. The types of imagery we have replaying in our mind's eye can be either positive or negative, with many variations in-between. Hypnosis is a great way to instil positive life-enhancing imagery for our subconscious to act upon and create as a reality. Whatever way we access these inner images is not what is important, as we are all able to recall from our inner world in a variety of ways that are uniquely ours.

Many people think they will not 'see' anything, so they doubt that hypnosis will work for them. However, using the imagination is a useful and powerful way to engage all of the senses to initiate change. This is what we want to take place, as the body will act on those images and turn them into reality. Hypnosis incorporates relaxation and the use of the imagination. The facilitator must also be relaxed and creatively use their own imagination to guide others. Using the creative part of the mind that is familiarly used even when daydreaming makes hypnosis feel natural and enjoyable for the client and practitioner.

When using the imagination we create without knowing how, imagery, even though we may not ordinarily think of ourselves as being visual. The imagination process involves using the natural clairvoyant ability we all have; visualising is part of the imagination that surfaces ideas spontaneously in the mind's eye. We imagine what we give our attention to, which is often an unconscious responsive act. When imagination incorporates feelings, the internal movement this creates activates our energy bodies or chakras, which function within their own vibrational fields and dimensions. Our awareness can tap in and utilise these energy bodies, as it travels inwards on various streams of consciousness.

Not everyone spontaneously sees images, but everyone can use their imagination to experience those informational fields and cause impressions to appear. You can test the client's suggestibility for accessing imagery, and let the client see how simple it is to relay images or impressions that come into the mind's eye and, more importantly, show them that they can do it. This dispels any anxiety about whether they are making things up.

They will be surprised and amazed at the ideas their imagination will show them in relation to what is going on below their conscious awareness. The SC has an incredible way of deciphering internal information, and it will provide the perfect visionary or sensory material for the client to experience and learn from. Whatever the client experiences will be entirely unique to that individual. The SC will bring forward information that is relevant and helpful to this present lifetime.

Our existence is an accumulation of our thoughts and

beliefs, which form emotionally driven perceptions that have their own stories. I don't follow the teachings of somatic or body-mind dictionaries as an absolute answer, but they can give some insights, however vague a starting point it may be. I personally believe that the reasons are more flexible than any standard guidelines. For this reason I don't recommend pre-suppositions about why a person is ill, as that would limit my thinking and narrow my level of awareness. I prefer to listen carefully and observe the client's verbal and body language. Core issues are deeply buried patterns of an energetic nature, and many link back to ancestral and genetic issues, which can be deeply rooted and often include learned behaviours. These energy patterns have a life of their own, and can gain unconscious strength by either our rejection of them, our disconnection from them, or our ability to suppress that which we fear most. Facing ourselves or looking deeply within takes great courage, as there are often many layers to peel back. Asking thought-provoking questions—rather than telling people what we think—will root out their truest feelings, their deepest hurts and their strongest desires. The SC will then reveal, with immaculate insight, the highest purpose and meaning that the client is able to receive at this time.

Deepeners

All hypnosis benefits from the use of deepeners, which is not so much about depth of trance state but more as a guide to prepare the mind to achieve better results. A deepener can be viewed as providing the client an opportunity of choosing to shift into a more desirable state. A good, effective script follows a certain pattern to allow for these natural deepening states, and should be flexible, as no two humans will respond to the same stimulus. When the higher levels come forward, a certain depth of trance is needed to bypass any conscious mind resistance to the unknown.

The best deepeners are natural things that cannot be resisted and don't engage the left-brain or conscious mind. The sound of the practitioner's voice or the client's voice will help deepen hypnosis. The breath is also an effective, natural deepener. At the very beginning of the session I embed the idea that all of the client's exhalations will deepen the state of relaxation. The left-brain cannot argue with such statements, which helps to maintain the 'yes' mind-set since the client will continue breathing and we will continue speaking. Any suggestion given, which is subjective in nature, engages the necessary or desired level of consciousness to carry out the suggestion.

The deepener can be as simple and casual as saying: "OK, now take a long deep breath, and as you exhale you will go deeper into that feeling. Now tell me what else you are noticing or experiencing." Allowing the client time and space to carry out any internal adjustments will deepen the mind's focus to carry out the task, which automatically alters the brain state and deepens the quality of trance. Sometimes, after a question is asked, the body inhales deeply as the consciousness drops down a few more levels. Then, as the client exhales and answers the question, you may notice a different tempo or pace as another aspect of the client becomes more prominent.

Not only is a deepener capable of deepening the trance state, but it also works as an intervention and a distraction from conscious mind interference. Anything that distracts the conscious can be used to take the client further within and deepen the trance. Opening and closing the eyes does this very effectively. Whenever we focus the client's attention on what is taking place within their body, it works as a deepener. Think about it this way: all internal focus is a deepener. With that in mind we are able to have them access their body through their feelings throughout the session, ensuring continuing deeper states of trance.

What is desired is the facilitation of a smooth transition from one state of being to another. We unconsciously use our imagination in response to the impressions we have of 'reality' as we perceive it. We can, however, intentionally reprogram those responses by identifying the original root cause, and make changes from the same level of mind that created it. Reframing the original cause effectively removes the original anchor while replacing it with the desired outcome.

This demonstrates the creative process of using whatever is at hand to deepen the hypnotic trance. This session tidbit begins with the first level of entering trance where the client is becomes internally engaged, and beginning to lose conscious awareness of their body.

(C) is the client (L) is myself.

C. *It's like swimming in water but I'm swimming in air.*

L. *How does it feel to swim in air... what does the air feel like?*

C. *I've had this feeling before, like when there is*

pressure around you... it's difficult to explain... when you are a tiny pinprick in the universe.

L. Take a deep breath and allow the feelings to continue building...

C. I feel sparks of energy and colours all around me. You know the pupil of an eye that has the coloured bits around it, and then those are like tentacles of colour shooting out everywhere. I can't quite describe it.

L. Well don't describe it, just enjoy it.

C. It's energy with variations of colour... highly magnified. I'm just floating with them and feel really tiny and all of this stuff is keeping me up, floating up.

My physical body is now feeling very heavy... although there is no weight to it or pressure to go anywhere but I could if I wanted to. (He still has body awareness so I know he is in high alpha and not fully yet in theta.)

L. Just allow that and detach from your body if you want to, and allow your consciousness to just float.

C. Before I got out of my body when you were sending me down deeper, I saw a matrix of energy and my body float out of my physical body... and that is where I found myself swimming. I can't see myself as anything, I'm just feeling myself.

L. Feel yourself in whatever way you want and let yourself drift deeper down to another level internally. The sound of my voice and the sound of your voice deepen your relaxation, in fact any sounds you hear inside the room or outside deepens your relaxation as you let yourself drift anywhere you like. The sound of my voice will follow you. Each time you take a breath and exhale everything becomes clearer until you have crystal clarity.

C. I'm now going down another level and I see crystals and many triangles. It's a place; I think... a land made of crystals. (He has now arrived into a significant experience.)

Analytical Types

Thinking any process through will activate the critical left-brain, causing it to analyse and compare. It is important to shift into the right brain or feelings in order to prevent any conscious mind intrusion. Feelings initiate an alpha state, and ideally you want the client to expand further into theta where they have no physical body awareness as they move deeply into consciousness awareness. This also removes the need for the client to feel forced into seeing things. The physical body awareness is great to explore during the pre-talk, but then you need to shift them away from that. There will be times during the SC healing when the client is focused on what is taking place within the body, but this is different from being consciously anchored inside the body through tension or concerns.

ADHD, ADD or Restless Clients

The restless mind can be very creative, as it is frequently in the alpha brainwave state and at least partially disconnected from body awareness. This type of personality is usually ungrounded. Making note of this will ensure that you take the time to add grounding techniques throughout the session. Speaking about hypnosis is, in itself, trance inducing, so it is beneficial to do so throughout the pre-talk rather than all at once before the formal induction. In fact, the technique of mini-inductions is beneficial for helping everyone attain a deeper trance state. Interspersing tidbits about what hypnosis is and does, phrasing bits and pieces as mini-inductions, while breathing smoothly and calmly helps the client to automatically slow their own breathing and mannerisms to match yours. This is another use of pacing and matching.

The mind that has a short interest or attention span is a naturally creative mind. This can work to our advantage if we work with it properly, rather than trying to get it to work with our way of thinking. Interspersing observational suggestions, alongside action suggestions such as doing, seeing, feeling and sensing, gives the client pause to pay attention and then respond. 'Doing' can include any action suggestion that requires their intuition, spontaneous thought response, or the use of their sensory attributes—including their telepathic ability to receive information. Breaking up the dialogue into bite-sized pieces enables such clients to shift from one topic or area of the body to another. The conversation should include questions such as: "What do you feel like doing now/about that/instead of ____?" etc. This allows the client to do whatever comes most easily and naturally to them. Guide the session in the direction of how their own mind naturally communicates with itself, and keep the client hypnotically engaged using the whole brain, both left and right hemispheres.

They will not need to be in a deep state of trance in order to have a successful session, as a deep trance state is not necessary to retrieve subconscious material for anyone. Explaining this in advance helps the client relax into the knowing that they can have a successful session, no matter what they may have believed previously. The deepener can be as simple and casual as saying, "Okay, now take a long deep breath, and as you exhale you will go deeper into that feeling. Now tell me what else you are noticing or experiencing." Then have them open their eyes again as you continue the pre-talk.

When working with restless clients who have short interest spans, it is best to use fractionation intermittently throughout the pre-talk. This will gradually relax the client, as each eye opening and closure exercise will build upon the last. If, for example, their eyes are closed as they access what is going on in their body, while speaking of emotional things, adding a deepener at that time will prepare them for the longer trance focus of hypnosis. This same approach can take place during trance, by instructing them that they can open their eyes at any time while still maintaining their deep relaxation/trance, and then when they close their eyes again, they will go twice as deep into peaceful relaxation than they were before. This gives them advance permission to know that they can relax deeper at any moment, and that they will not have to worry about having a successful session. As for the formal induction it is best to keep it brief, or better still, to use a rapid induction.

The Voice

The sound of our voice is powerful for trance induction. It was discovered in the 1970s that certain musical tempos keep the brain alert while learning new things as the body sleeps. While shamans drum, various other spiritual practices chant, or use other mind or body altering movements to achieve this same mind state. Hypnosis is very effective spoken in a normal voice, as we see stage hypnotists demonstrate, but for therapeutic work it is better to be soothing and conversational when speaking with the client, rather than speaking at them. The client remains connected to the external world through the sound of your voice and their own voice. Also a hypnotic, rhythmic flow is instrumental in igniting and guiding the client's imagination, as it journeys toward locating the most appropriate information to be brought forward at this time.

The Imaginary Jump-start

Sometimes it is necessary to actively use the imagination to jump-start the inner journey, which will move the client into non-physical realities where they can access unconscious mind revelations. Pretending stimulates the imagination, and the imagination is the gateway into the non-physical worlds. These worlds are held together as reality consensus systems. The practitioner's role is to become a skilful guide and storyteller — not because we tell the stories, but because we know how to allow the stories the space they need to be heard and acknowledged. Exercising the imagination and directing its point of focus opens up inner dimensions that are not consciously available to us. Rather than describing something that does not come to mind easily, pretending kick-starts the natural daydreaming ability and shifts awareness from the left to the right brain, or from alpha to theta. This moves the client deeper into dreamlike symbolic language and imagery. As the senses become fully engaged, impressions and perceptions unfold, and the switchover is so smooth that the client doesn't even realise they have become fully engaged in a way they may not have expected.

Many of our fears are formed in our imagination, as well as the antidotes for them. Imagination is more than just daydreaming; it is a tool for communication and interaction with the non-physical realms. In esoteric traditions the astral planes are known as the planes of the imagination, an indication of how entwined imagination, manifestation and creation are. Discovering how a client uses their imagination can be very insightful in showing us how they think about what goes on in their head. As children, we were often scolded for daydreaming by adults, which causes many not to recognise the benefits of using their imagination to their advantage. We often don't trust it or think of its use for only creating fantasy, but it is much more than that.

Our nightly dreams confirm that our dream life, while taking place, is every bit as real as our physical life. It's easy to struggle with the idea that our imagination must be making up these subconscious revelations, as our conscious mind lacks the expanded imagery and awareness that the subconscious has, so the conscious mind may expect to experience things as though through physical eyes. It is important to remember that unlike our dream world, in which the conscious mind is asleep, a client can view multiple layers, dimensions and aspects of their entire being or higher self.

The Conscious Mind is Always in the Background

The conscious mind does not leave or go anywhere. It remains present in the background as the observer, just as the SC is always in the background recording data. Consciousness is able to parallel process, and during a session this can cause a dreamlike feeling of duality. Wherever awareness is focused is where the light of attention shines, and that spotlight of awareness becomes the primary supplier of information. As we shift our awareness, different aspects of information are seen and become available.

The conscious mind stays in the background when

the brain is in hypnosis, carrying on its own inner dialogue about whatever it is paying attention to. It may be thinking that the visuals or information are so far removed from its ordinary daily experiences that the client is just imagining things, or it may be noticing that it has never quite thought about or viewed things in the way they are being presented now. The conscious mind doesn't usually interfere during hypnosis, unless there is an emotional reason for resisting change that creates an inner struggle or conflict.

Conscious Mind Intrusion

If the conscious mind intrudes it will begin to rationalise through logic, whereas the SC is not inhibited by structured analysis and can intuitively engage in free flowing imagery and impressions in a dreamlike, seemingly random way. However, when looked at collectively the ideas presented are not random at all, as there are themes that have emotional and psychological importance and meaning to the client. We willingly use our conscious mind to think, but the SC communicates with us through our feelings. Guiding the client deeper into the body or feelings deepens trance, increases insight and creates a foundation for permanent healing.

The client may speak of doubts during the process. If this happens there's no need to become frustrated or try to engage in discussion about it. Simply agree with what is said using your induction voice. In other words, maintain your pace, and calmly say: "Okay, leave that behind for now and take a nice deep breath, and as you exhale slowly... (add your suggestion or question)."

Don't become argumentative, staying calm and agreeing with them keeps them in a 'yes' mind-set, and they will still follow your guidance without analysis or critique.

An Example of CM intrusion

Conscious mind resistance throughout the session does not always imply that the exploration won't be successful. Jenny had 'a fear of going to hell' that prevented her from living her life and enjoying things that others did.

Her special place was a forest where she immediately saw a path with sunlight at the end of it. Going down it she discovers that it is a ball of light like the sun. She floats up to it and then tells me she's still very aware of the surroundings in our room. I tell her that she can let all of that go and that a part of her can stay here in the room and another part of her can float up to investigate the light if she wants to. She now tells me that she's immersed in the ball of light. She tells me repeatedly that she's finding it very hard to not be aware of her physical surroundings, and that she can't do the session as she is consciously aware of being there in the room. I tell her that she can give that part of herself permission to be aware of her surroundings if it needs to, and to let it know there is no need to sabotage this experience... that it can observe if it wants to and share its thoughts with her after.

She now begins to describe herself as a young nun, and is shown a variety of significant scenes including taking pledges. When she later died she drifts away from her body into the dark. Once again she tells me how her

CM is involved and just won't go away. Thinking quickly I intuitively ask her if she can relocate the nun and she does and we get her permission to ask questions. She asks if her fear of going to hell is connected to her, the nun, who confirms that yes, she has taken oaths and made pledges. We then ask her if she is ready to be released from them. These 'contracts' that the client/nun has made are removed and the client is given "a very nice warm feeling." The lifetime as a nun has been influencing the client, preventing her from doing many fun things and these are now addressed and healed. Some of these imageries are quite unique and detailed yet still the client constantly says her awareness is still in the room, etc. As these things take place the client describes all the physical feelings and sensations she's feeling including the increased feelings of them I ask for. (I do this so that she can have no doubts that something is taking place.) She tells me again that she is aware of the traffic outside so I tell her that a part of her mind can drift outside with the traffic if it wants to and the other parts of her can pull themselves together here.

She sends out the thought to the nun to let her know that she is ready to have them reintegrated, that she needs all the skills and the awareness that the nun has learned in that lifetime. She tells her that she is grateful for the nuns learning but it's time now to be integrated with her. The nun is now crying at Jenny's feet (an example of two soul aspects communicating as individual personalities) because she "is scared of hell." We reassure her that there is no hell and that her pledge was man-made which she has left behind. The client feels a 'connectedness' now taking place with her and the nun as they begin integrating. Different colours present themselves to remove the residual effects of the nun that were affecting the client.

She tells me now about the chattering of her conscious mind, I tell her to just let that go for now and let's get the nun healed so that she cannot influence her anymore and can be at peace.

A little patience keeps the facilitator in a relaxed frame of mind to be inspired no matter what the client's hesitation or 'resistance' may be. Through perseverance, the client was able to find the originating causes of her 'problems' and receive healing. I went so far as to agree with whatever she said about her conscious mind being present thus keeping her in a 'yes' mind-set. I calmly showed her that other parts of herself can multitask and function simultaneously without telling her how this could be possible. The details of the nun that unfolded were significant in relation to her current life and it addressed all of her concerns. Her questions were answered, she saw imagery and experienced other sensory input while still listening to traffic outside and constantly interrupting to speak from her analytical mind.

The nun, like Jenny, was an aspect of their shared soul who was stuck somewhere in the consciousness spectrum holding onto beliefs that were affecting Jenny's life. With their integration Jenny can benefit from the skills, knowledge and experiences that the nun can contribute to their collective group consciousness, and more importantly she will no longer have the adverse reactions created by the nun's fears and beliefs. The integration will allow both to unite, create wholeness and well being, and more importantly be able to bring the collective energy into more harmony or balance.

Breathing

When a client experiences conscious mind intrusion or self-doubt, a breathing intervention is useful. Using your soothing induction voice, you could say: "Okay, just let that go for now and take a nice deep, slow breath and, as you exhale, (add what you want to occur)" or, "Okay, breathing in deeply, allow your consciousness/awareness to ____," or, "I wonder how it would be if you just drifted away from that scene, knowing you can come back to it later." In other words, as you acknowledge what they are feeling or saying, you don't engage them mentally but shift their awareness back to the breathing process. When the left-brain becomes engaged, their breathing becomes shallower and they are less relaxed, so it is beneficial if you use their breath as a deepener. You can consistently bring them back to their breath if need be, when they are not seeing or voicing any impressions. You can use breathing to help them see or know things: "Taking a deep breath and exhaling slowly, you will know ____ or remember ____."

At the very beginning I suggest to them that their exhalations deepen their relaxation. It can be very interesting to watch as the session progresses. Sometimes after they are asked a question they inhale deeply, go down a few notches, exhale, and then answer the question.

Deep breathing is very important. We naturally relax when we exhale, so besides being a deepener it can be used as a means of accessing previously unknown information, on the client's exhalation.

The challenge as practitioner is to not say anything intrusive, while using the client's breathing as an involuntary process to access deep relaxation, and also maintaining the 'yes' mind-set. Nobody ever resists breathing deeply.

When Clients Think They Are Not Visual

The following technique I learned from one of my teachers, Dr. Raymond Roberts at The Elestial Training School (UK) when studying advanced hypnotherapy, and can be easily adapted to suit the interest of each person, for example using other objects such as musical things or a musician, or things in nature of the outdoor person:

If a client thinks they are not visual have them think of a small ball or use an object that is relevant to their lifestyle, and then proceed by having them visually transform the shape of the object. For example you could say: "Imagine a small ball. Now allow that image to fade away as it becomes a football. Allow that image to fade away as it turns into a beach ball." Repeat the image changing and fading away several times. Each time the client changes the image, reinforce them by having them describe the new object in detail. Encourage them by saying something like: "See you can visualise and the more you do it the easier it gets."

After that first little exercise move on to this one: Ask the client to locate a time when they were a child, then a teenager, a young adult, etc. Ask them to respond with a simple 'yes' when they locate each time. After they confirm it, encourage them to speak about it, by saying things like: "Tell me about it...tell me more about what that was like." Then ask them to locate a certain kind of place and have them tell you about what that place is like. Or you can run the timeline in the opposite direction by asking about something that happened last week, last year, a few years ago, as a teenager; then explain to the client that this is how they will experience the session. Sometimes things, people and events will seem especially clear and defined while others may not, but this is completely natural. Remind the client that you will be asking questions throughout the session, and that they simply need to verbalise the first impressions and sensations that come into their awareness.

The goal is to help the client feel comfortable and confident in their ability to receive and respond. Whatever way an answer comes to them is perfect, as it does not matter how the information is relayed as long as they allow it to surface. They only need to tell you whatever it is that they are seeing, sensing and experiencing. Let them know in advance that some imagery may be clearer than others, and this will reinforce their understanding that they don't have to be an expert at visualising.

Exercising the imagination and directing its point of focus opens up inner dimensions that are not consciously available to us. Rather than describing something that does not come to mind easily, pretending kick-starts the natural daydreaming ability and shifts awareness from the left to the right brain, or from alpha to theta. This moves the client deeper into dreamlike symbolic language and imagery. As the senses become fully engaged, impressions and perceptions unfold, and the switchover is so smooth that the client doesn't even realise they have become fully engaged in a way they may not have expected.

Body Jerks or Involuntary Motions

When the parasympathetic nervous system relaxes, tension gets released from the body, which may cause reactive jerks or minor tremors. You might already have noticed that when sleeping beside someone else, their body twitches or jerks when falling asleep. When this happens spontaneously during the pre-talk, it can be used as a Somatic Bridge to access underlying feelings and the original cause of that reaction. There are other times throughout the session when body movements are likely to happen, such as during an energetic healing or as the client merges with higher vibrational frequencies.

Healing energies moving through the body may also create changes in body temperature, shaking or vibrating, coughing, crying, sighing, smiling or even laughing aloud. Just stay open and curious, allowing the body to release its hold on the client's psyche. Continue exploring what is taking place without judgment, and have the client share with you the details of what they are experiencing.

When it comes to changes occurring through a change in breathing, it may be that the client is deepening to another level of trance before responding from a higher level of consciousness, especially when it occurs after being asked a question. But if, however, the breathing becomes erratic or the client begins hyperventilating, it may be a huge emotional release erupting. Abreactions can be very powerful forms of release, but not every practitioner is comfortable following through with them, unless they have developed confidence in this area.

Bridge Techniques

The Bridge Technique is an excellent process that is used successfully to induce trance naturally. Through describing then experiencing strong suppressed emotions (preferably with closed eyes), while focusing on the feelings and imagined ideas, the mind bridges back to the original event though unconscious memories or events. The Bridge involves high feelings of emotion, like anger or fear — the most consistently suppressed emotions arise and are released and expressed, and the client may become emotional. Saying the first impressions that come to mind begins deepening the trance state that must now be stabilised. They do this by engaging all their senses, just the same as when describing a 'special place', by describing what are they seeing, sensing, feeling and aware of, as this will fully integrate them into the experience.

When researching past life material, integrate the client into the scene by asking questions like: "About how old do you feel? Please describe your body. What gender are you?" etc. Sometimes the SC will reveal information from an earlier time in the current lifetime.

When practitioners are afraid of strong emotions they prevent the client from expressing them, which means they will only be able to touch upon the surface of what their deeper problems or emotions might be. Some practitioners value their own comfort more than their client's discomfort, but to be effective they must be able to work with clients when they are experiencing and expressing strong emotions. It is recommended that practitioners try many self-exploratory sessions as the 'client' themselves, to clear their own stuff and refine their skills. This prevents transference and other unconscious projections that are linked to trying to rescue clients.

Affect Bridge

An Affect Bridge is formed when clients identify with strong emotional content. You guide the client by asking them to intensify the feelings in the body. Using circular repetitive comments phrased slightly differently to bypass their CM will assist them to go beneath the surface to connect with the underlying stories. You could say: "You can go deeper into it than that. What are the feelings behind that?" Time must be given for this process to unfold, so ask them to share with you whatever impressions arise. If you integrate them into the imagery, this deepens the trance and opens up more revelations.

Linguistic Bridge

It may be that they used a particular phrase to sum up how they feel, which can be used as a Linguistic Bridge. In this the practitioner says: "Close your eyes and repeat that phrase over and over, feeling it more intensely, and then share with me the first things that come to mind."

Somatic Bridge

Using a Somatic Bridge or the feelings within the body is somewhat rare, but this consists of connecting a physical experience to its origin.

I find that using a combination of breath, with an Affect or Linguistic Bridge, is an effective rapid induction.

Going to a Specific Time or Event

If the aim is to resolve a traumatic situation or explore specific events, then the starting point of the exploration is directing the client to locate the time before the event occurred, then gently guide them to discover, "What happens next?" You can direct them to a specific date, year, event or whatever is most appropriate. For example, should a client feel they may have been abducted or experienced missing time, let them know that if they wish, they can review this with curiosity, as an observer. Let them know that they do not actually need to experience the event again, because they have already survived whatever took place in the past.

The Special, Sacred or Beautiful Place

The beginning of the hypnosis, in which the client is guided to experience a 'special place' allows them to go to a safe, peaceful, relaxing place within their mind. This adds to their overall comfort level.

The special place, used to induce inner exploration, is best suggested as a natural environment, perhaps somewhere in nature that the client has already been to, or an imaginary place that comes to mind as being comfortable and peaceful. Two things take place here: first they can describe a familiar place, which helps those who fear they may not be visual, and second it allows the client to enter a state of mind that is an enjoyable, relaxing environment in which people don't feel the need to activate defences.

We can also suggest that it does not necessarily have to be in nature, just a very special or sacred place for them, wherever they feel most peaceful. Their description will cleverly anchor them into the scene or setting, as they use their inner senses to gather impressions. This is all right-brain activity, and will easily put the left analytical brain aside, as they access feelings and sensations.

Quantum journeys can begin from any place of peace and comfort, as you can incorporate creative ways to move the client forward from that point. It is not necessary to use the word 'magical', but I prefer to use it myself, as the mind will more readily accept anything unusual or similar to the dreaming state. For example, if the client finds themselves in the woods, at a beach, or on a mountain there are always pathways, clouds, boats or other things that can be used to create a deeper movement inward and a conclusion upon arrival. Should clients find themselves within a building, there are doorways, windows, elevators or stairs that can be used to lead them to another timeline.

As mentioned before, the special place is a standard hypnotherapy deepener that is introduced just after the induction at the beginning of the session. In truth, the special place can itself induce one into trance, as it is a natural deepening technique that solidifies inner sensory focus in a way that causes people to feel relaxed and peaceful. Establishing inner focus and an overall sense of wellbeing is important. For these same reasons, the special place can be used again at any time during the session when there are high emotions, an abreaction, excessively fearful feelings or the need to move a stuck session forward. At other times, when there is conscious mind interference, I'll send that part of them back to continue enjoying their special place. Whenever we do this we must remember to reintegrate them again before the completion of the session.

Sensing Through the Feelings

As electromagnetic beings our feelings have a frequency value, as information streams of consciousness holding all of our history. Connecting or communicating through our senses and feelings with these vibrational frequencies begins the process of self-awareness, and leads to the discovery of deep and powerful insights. Helping the client to feel and acknowledge what those vibrations are is an excellent way to release, heal and increase awareness. Fears can be seen for what they really mean, instead of the many guises the conscious mind wears to cloak, hide or repress them. This is where true knowing, self-empowerment, and the connecting of the dots are initiated.

The 12 Guiding Concepts

This guide is from QHHT practitioner, Missy Sorrels, to help clients anchor into their beautiful place and deepen the trance state:

General Information (the 3Ws)
1) WHAT: asking what things, people, buildings, etc, that the client is sensing.
2) WHERE: getting a context or environment

around what the client is sensing.

3) WHEN: this can be general timeframe. Does the client sense day or night, morning or evening, birth or death, etc?

Adding details (the 4Ss):

4) SIZE: things seen such as buildings, landscape, animals, people, etc.

5) SHAPE: are things seen round, triangular, oval, arched, etc?

6) SOUND: what is the client hearing? Voices, nature sounds, city sounds, etc.

7) SMELLS: environmental, etc.

More details (the 2Cs):

8) COLOUR: client describes colours of things around them, on them, etc.

9) CONDITIONS: is the client hot or cold, tired or energetic, healthy or sick, poor or wealthy, kind or mean, light or dark, wet or dry, etc.

Additional details: (M.A.N.):

10) MOOD: is the mood of self or others angry, happy, frustrated, joyful, etc.

11) ACTION: what is happening? Are any movement or events happening?

12) NUMBER: of people, animals, buildings, etc.

Allowing the Process of Self-Discovery

As we allow ourselves to tap into these infinite fields of information we move beyond time as we would ordinarily experience it, and this enables us to explore any number of other timelines that also exist.

As we step outside of time we step into the unusual, and what we experience may seem nonsensical to our more practical conscious mind, which may not have conscious reference points to associate with ideas or experiences from other timelines. However, rest assured, the SC will clearly reveal and explain the data brought forward, down to the most minute and subtle detail.

Communicating in the Present Tense

For healing, or change in general, we must always communicate in the present tense. Don't use indefinite words such as try, hope, could, should and wish; using ideas that include action and progressive change unites the client with that reality. When we work with the mind we don't need to distinguish what level or layer of it we need to address. Suggestions and thoughts, when accepted, take place quickly. However, to prevent any resistance on the part of the conscious mind, it is best to be repetitive with those suggestions. Significant keywords reinforce ideas, especially if they hold emotional value that can replace any undesirable, currently-held emotional beliefs. The quality of word choice and the language we use can build and deepen trust, and stop the client being tense. Reassuring words reinforce and achieve positive outcomes.

We must know when to switch to present tense, help with movement geared towards self-discovery, identify and release previous anchors, and learn not to lead the client in any way to support our own concepts. If the aim is simply curiosity for the sake of consciousness exploration that may be fine, but for more serious illnesses that need healing more is called for from the practitioner, in order to guide the client to necessary solutions. Temporary relief comes with all sessions, but more is called for when a permanent healing is desired, as the end goal needs a thorough excavation of the feelings, ideas and past traumas held in the body that need releasing. Whatever the past life patterns were, we now know that they are still an active on-going stream of consciousness, still affecting and influencing the client in real time.

There really is no past, as we continuously live out beliefs and anchors contained within the psyche in the present time. Using present-tense language is important, as this reveals evolving storylines, and explains how the client connects those stories with various parts of the body-soul matrix. We need to work in a transformative manner rather than observational one, and this involves engaging the entire being, rather than just the thinking aspect. We want them to know, rather than just see. This is the way that true healing can be stabilised.

Information Gathering- during hypnosis

Developing our own style can take a bit of practise, as it has to be natural and comfortable. If we are comfortable then we can rest assured that the client is too. I particularly prefer a very casual conversational tone, as that removes the interrogational style that can often engage left-brained responses or interactions. The key is to never allow the conscious mind to communicate directly with us during hypnosis; it had its turn in the pre-talk and understands that it now needs to step aside now the client is suitably relaxed. The conscious mind is always there observing and is quite happy doing so unless it is drawn into the discussion, because the client begins analysing or criticising what is taking place from a point of ego or the 'I' stance. This is different from explaining what is being seen or experienced from the subconscious mind.

Keep it simple: One of the most effective and simplest of techniques is to repeat what the client has just said, but add a questioning tone or inflection. Feeding back their comments to them with a slight pause allows them to elaborate further. This is a favourite method of mine, as I do not have to think in advance, lead or guide them anywhere. I simply show them that I am listening, which encourages them to continue adding more detail. In reality I am subtly drawing out more information in a very relaxed manner, and I also feed back to them the exact words they used in the pre-talk. When they are describing emotive subjects during the talk they are very specific in the language they use. I make a note of these as they are a bridge to an emotional event or situation that are almost always due to decisions they may have made on the last day of a previous life, or the underpinning of a life growth or lesson situation.

Open-ended questions encourage a dialogue: We get far more information when answers are not restricted to yes or no. Closed-ended questions can only ever provide incomplete information, such as why something is a yes or no does not get discussed, or add any further insight. This can be likened to the difference between knowledge and wisdom.

When asking them if they want to do something in particular, it can be phrased as: "If you like you can

____," or, "I wonder what would happen if you decided to ____?"

Be Curious: To get the most out of the session we have to become curious, and imagine we are a spiritual journalist with the aim to get the most high-quality information around the questions the client has. Why get a partial story when it takes the same time and effort to get the full story? It is not enough to read the script and expect the session to deliver the results you would like; the script only takes them into the story, but the finer details come about through the discussion that ensues. It is the quality of questions and dialogue that provide the greatest depth and insight. Think of the initial SC answer to a question as the heading of a paragraph, and with skilful guidance we can get them to reveal more content to add body to the paragraph—now you have an evolving commentary that can unfold in its own way. This approach guides them deeper into trance as they become more focused internally.

Following through on what has been stated by the client is imperative: exploration or excavation allows the layers to get peeled away to reveal the wisdom buried within. Metaphorically speaking, it can be likened to creating a solid foundation on which to build your house. This prevents generic assumptions on the practitioner's part when the answers are vague that 'it must have been their first life', or 'the SC knows best', if you are not getting any detailed results. We must dig deeper into what is being shared with us, to help clients validate and connect all the dots in their life. There's no point sending them away with as many questions as they came with or incomplete information. Providing them with as much precise information as possible helps them to expand their awareness permanently. It also prevents them from questioning the validity of the session and thinking they must be making it up. Digging further into the details will lead to a perfect fit in explaining their life questions.

This type of layered information gathering is helpful for the clients, as they are not in a position to ask their own questions and removes self-doubt in trance; they need us to help them clear away the surface debris. Only they can validate their commentary to their own satisfaction after the session. Perhaps, like me, you may have been in a situation as the client, in which you wanted the facilitator to explore something further and they just moved on, not realising that what has been said would benefit from further exploration. This can be very frustrating, as not all clients are able to just speak and offer information without being asked. It is important that we note subtle or casual statements made during the pre-talk to see how they are connecting with what is being revealed through hypnosis, and when appropriate have them expand on it.

Stabilise the scene: There is a need to stabilise what they are experiencing by helping them to become fully engaged in the experience and their impressions, so they can acquire accurate details. This limits the 'I don't know' response, and applies even if they are the observer and not feeling overwhelming emotions. Think of yourself as watching a movie, and being able to note all the details on the screen.

Listen carefully and limit your speech: Remember we have two ears and one mouth for a reason, meaning we don't need to make too many comments. It's far more important to listen and encourage the clients to talk, express and release their information; all that's required of us is to encourage and ensure the client knows they are being heard. Sometimes we get caught up with wanting to speak too much or express our 'wisdom' and insight. However, it is more beneficial to save such comments for the post-talk, if and when appropriate. The clients are not with us to hear what we think, but for us to help them discover what THEY unconsciously think and feel. The key here is to ask questions, but not tell the clients what we think. It is imperative that we follow up on things they initiate.

Make no assumptions: Be aware of any assumptions you may have by asking yourself if your questions are based on what you feel, or what the client has said in the pre-talk or during hypnosis. Even if we think we know what the client is seeing or saying, we cannot determine the veracity of that, and we should never project our beliefs onto them. What you assume to be logical may be untrue for the client, and we risk leading them away from their SC's guidance. And if a client is not forthcoming with past life information it does not follow it is their first life here. Also, first timers are not always 'volunteers.' Earth life is constantly attracting souls who wish to grow, and it stands to reason that newcomers are always coming into life here.

Sometimes our own curiosity wants us to shift the conversation in a particular way, but it may be out of the natural flow of what is being directed from a higher perspective. Many times after a session we may think about questions we could have asked, but they did not flow into the dialogue naturally for a reason. If it doesn't flow then it's our ego or insecurity introducing what we feel should have been said. There is a delicate balance between introducing a new direction without enforcing our own will. As a general rule, if we have to think too hard about inserting what we want, then there is a subconscious urge telling us not to. We cannot make assumptions about the comments as they are revealed, but must dig deeper for greater clarification and insight.

Clarification: We only get as much information as we are willing to encourage. Sometimes the client is very vague with their answers, as the information has yet to unfold and is slow in coming forward. In such instances it is necessary to help them clarify by asking them: "What exactly do you mean when you say ___?" If they can't answer easily, or they hesitate too long, then we can always tell them to breathe deeply, and as they exhale they will know the answer. Focusing on the breath prevents the conscious mind from becoming engaged, and it allows the answer to pop into their awareness. Sometimes I deliberately paraphrase incorrectly, so they will correct me and provide more detailed information.

Don't interrupt the flow: It's also important not to interrupt, as this often breaks the client's flow and may lead them somewhere other than where their SC wants to go. If we find we are speaking at the same time, it is helpful to stop, and ask them to repeat and elaborate on what they were saying. (Of course, if they are talking too much during the pre-talk, then any interruption can be of benefit.)

Silence is always golden: Silence or gaps in conversation can work to our advantage. It is helpful to learn to sit with the silence, to allow the client the space needed to formulate what they are sensing, and then express it in their own time. Sometimes a very talkative session becomes lengthy because of pauses waiting for the SC to come through, which may cause some anxiety on your part.

When learning to sit with silence we can also increase our own sensory abilities and discover far more from the client through observation. We can use the time to become aware of any non-verbal information, such as REM, the mouth silently moving, or other muscular movements — those are clear signs that something is occurring. We may need to ask them to share what they are experiencing with us, to have it recorded for their future reference and to break the pause.

Silence is also a great time to match and pace our energy with the clients, which deepens their trance state. Remember that our energy naturally interacts in some way with others in our environment. Sometimes when you feel the silence has been too long and start to speak, so does the client. This is a clear sign that there was something occurring and patience is necessary. Silence creates holes that will need to be filled, providing far more information, so it may be that after a lengthy silence you can either repeat your question or introduce another. We can become self-aware by periodically asking ourselves how comfortable we are with silence — if we are not comfortable then the client will subconsciously sense it and feel pressured, which engages their left brain or conscious mind with self-critique.

Interventions

The conscious mind sometimes interferes during trance when there is an emotional attachment to the topic being discussed, or when there is resistance to letting go completely — which can lighten the trance. This shows us that people will not do the bidding of others when in trance if it goes against their personal beliefs.

Attachment to outcomes is a function of the conscious mind, which views its role as maintaining the status quo in daily life. This may not seem so obvious if a client comes to you and says they want healing. Keep in mind that there may be payoffs, consciously or subconsciously, for remaining unwell. In such cases a subtle intervention may be all that's needed to allow the client to move deeper into the trance state. Interventions to identify fears can help the client shift internally into SC communication, creating a smooth transition back to the 'yes' mind-set. The pre-talk should explore the core issues and beliefs of the client, primarily to allow the SC to initiate solutions and make lasting changes in problematic areas.

Using interventions is a simple way to reinforce the focusing process before proceeding. It also helps to increase relaxation while stimulating the imagination. This takes the client outside time or space, which is necessary for hypnosis to occur.

Body Scans

These can be carried out at any time during the session. Closing the eyes and noticing any feelings in the body when speaking about emotive topics begins the process. You could, therefore ask: "What, if anything, do you notice when you scan your body?" or simply, "What does that feel like?" During hypnosis body scans can be carried out by the subconscious mind, spirit guides, helpers, healers, 'friends' and any other non-physical beings that become a part of the session and work on behalf of the client's well-being. The same things can be questioned and resolved by the SC, collective higher mind and various other levels of consciousness. It's not surprising that both processes—specific exploration and the body scan—might be undertaken with differing qualities of information around the same topics, depending on who or what level of consciousness is undertaking the scan. Have the client detail as much as possible what occurs at this time.

Spiritual Tune-Up

A spiritual tune-up should consist of, among other things:
• Opening the energy flow in the meridians, or imagining 'rivers of light' running through the body.
• Requesting that all chakras be rebalanced.
• Asking for all body systems to be operating at their peak levels, such as endocrine, digestive, etc.
• Releasing all energy blocks or imbalances.
• Releasing toxins within the organs of the body or mind.
• Checking for any leakage points in the auric field and requesting correction.
• Asking that the heart and all cells in the body be filled with unconditional self-love.

We should check that all is well and harmoniously in balance within the body and its systems. Neville, came for a session as he has cancer. His higher self recommended a whole change in lifestyle and a renewal of his commitment to being connected to earth and natural things. He was told that with "nature, when it can't read you it sets out to destroy you as it doesn't recognise you... it needs to be able read me as a part of everything else within nature. It's for humanity to be connected to nature in that way."

"If we disconnect ourselves, nature cannot read us or give us what we need. If we are connected we are like the bears and other animals and nature can read us then, and provide for us what we need to maintain good health, as it provides for all the other animals naturally. We think we need to provide for ourselves, but we don't, nature provides for us, and makes us a part of all natural creation. But we've kind of set ourselves apart, thinking that, we've got ourselves, and then we've got nature. We can't separate ourselves from nature by thinking that 'the laws of the jungle' do not apply to us, because we're not animals, because we are. Then we try and create a facade around us with man-made things that are unnatural, but really it is just us being be IN nature but in a disconnected way, as there is nothing but nature. When we are connected to nature it reads us and when we are open to being read by the rest of nature it can provide for us in abundance.

"If we disconnect ourselves and put ourselves on the 50th floor of a building, it's hard for nature to read us. If you're tottering around in high heels in a man-made environment, it's hard for nature to get to you. If your feet are close to the floor and you are in nature, nature can read what you need and what your desires are. Then nature can put the opportunities in front of you, where you can acquire or access those things. We need to take a step towards accepting those things though, by holding them, and saying thank you for them. It's not foisted upon us, but it's presented similar to the way nature presents fruits (from the plants). It's not always (going to be) there, but it comes, and it's for us to reach out to it. We can say thank you, and accept it, and, 'I can see why nature has given this to me because I can use it and I accept it wholeheartedly.'"

Persistence

Persistence does not mean moving forward in an aggressive, directive manner, but rather calmly following through on anything that takes place. When a client makes a comment during hypnosis—for example stating that something can't be done—it may simply mean that more information gathering and detail is necessary, so it's important to leave no question unanswered. Persistence is also needed at times to negotiate for healing, and an example would be if the SC says it cannot perform the healing that has been requested. It is best if we approach whatever is said with scepticism because doing so allows us to be more thorough in our questioning and in gathering detail. We get the best results by approaching our questioning from a variety of angles, which results in more clarity for both client and practitioner—without prejudice or assumption.

Removing Barriers

Walls can be symbolic of resistance or intense fears, and they can be reduced brick by brick, which serves the purpose of a hypnotic deepener.

You could say: "In a moment I'm going to ask you to remove the bricks one at a time by first imagining the brick in your mind's eye and then, by using that wonderful imagination of yours, I want you to see them dissolving or disintegrating in whatever way you choose. And as it disappears you will become twice as deeply relaxed as you are now. With each brick you dissolve I'd like you to breathe in deeply and exhale slowly, and that will be my cue to know that you are moving on to dissolve the next brick. By the time you have done this three times you will have dissolved the entire wall. Then I would like you to tell me the first thing you become aware of, and each time you exhale it deepens your relaxation, as you become more and more confident, comfortable, relaxed and settled." You can have them make a doorway in the wall, or get really creative as you provide an activity to engage the conscious mind in a constructive way. This allows it to hand those directions to their subconscious, right brain creative self, to carry out the task. This is a circular way of engaging the right brain away from any guarded left-brain limitations.

Resistance

It might seem that there is a conscious reason for resisting, but I've found that there is usually a deep seated or imagined fear, with its roots somewhere in the past. Issues cannot be directly forced into awareness. Instead, explore what is being felt as they resist or avoid, and go behind the feeling to discover its voice. We cannot make assumptions about why there is resistance, or press our points of view upon the client, as doing so would be counterproductive to self-realisation. When accessing a space that connects them to intense feelings they may seem fearful at first. We can't make assumptions, but we must stay in a loving place, reassuring the client that all is well, and remind them that they can choose to observe or review things from a distance if they wish.

Often intense feelings can surface unconsciously, and this may occur shortly after the induction. Ask: "What is the fear behind the resistance? What are the feelings that are taking place in the body? What words come to mind when you focus on the feelings?" Find out as much as you can. If there is no further movement away from the resistance, then a bridge can be used to discover the original feeling. There is always a way around things if we work with the client's perception or level of consciousness, rather than trying to get them to do what we think is best.

Soul Loss and Fragmentation

The soul can be thought of as the immortal, eternal part of ourselves that keeps us alive, which is directly expressing our spiritual essence and does not die with the body. It's the part of us that connects to all other aspects, is the holder of all experiences, intentions and lessons, and the outcomes of those experiences. Sometimes emotional pieces of us become lost, split off or stuck in a past life, not realising that it has transitioned through death and needs to be re-integrated. If there are lost souls connected to the client that need to cross into the light, this should always take place with compassion and not fear.

Soul loss occurs throughout our childhood as a coping mechanism. In order to prevent becoming overwhelmed we bury our feelings, which fragments parts of our soul's available energy. Such disconnects deplete us over time, and can become the leading cause of physical ailments and disease. One of the best ways to raise the vibrational energy field is to undergo energy clearing and regeneration. The unconscious communicates its messages through the body as feelings of comfort or discomfort. The body does not lie — it is always reflecting whatever is going on inwardly. So the body can be used to confirm the energy exchanges and responses that occur on the inner realms as physical sensations, especially when healing is taking place.

In matters of soul loss, when recalling soul fragments they should return to the client as something beautiful or pleasing, rather than dark. Their return enhances the client's energy, adding vitality and an increase in conscious self-awareness. Clients have described soul fragments as butterflies, crystals, light, glass-like shards and colours coming back into the body. You needn't ask if any soul parts have been fragmented, as through a soul's journey of experience in an emotional world like ours, thoughts and feelings impact us on the emotional level daily. Given enough energy, thought forms, as attachments to things, create a duality and a splitting off of self—and that's only on this dimension! It is likely that on any soul's journey fragmentation does occur, in order to allow stories to be created.

Understanding or locating individual soul fragments is unnecessary and time-consuming as they can return collectively, not just from past lives, but also from the multiverse or universe. This is because many souls have had lives in different galaxies and systems that are beyond our human understanding, or they may have had many past Earth lives with active psychic connections from interacting with others.

After releasing undesired attachments and obtaining freedom from past agreements, clearing and cleansing the cells and energies will raise the client's vibration, stabilise a new foundation and establish a new reality. Major releases are felt internally and externally.

Famous Personality Reincarnations

Many people describe having the same famous personality in a past life as others, which may or not be authentic. There are many theories about this.

The best one I have found that resonates with me is that of Dr. Shakuntala Modi, in her book *Memories of God and Creation: Remembering from the Subconscious Mind*. Using diagrams, her hypnotised patients draw a picture of how souls in the vicinity of those famous souls absorb their energy and experiences, feeling as though it is personal to them.

There is no more value in a life that is famous compared to one that is not; they are just individual lives in a stream of many. Besides being influenced by books, movies or imaginary ideas that may influence the session, archetypal energies can present themselves in sessions: Isis, Merlin or other mythological beings do come to interact at times. Clients describe these beings from a first-person perspective or from participating in ceremonies in their honour, but do not always use their name, just their description. This may be due to the level of their lives being described, in that they are just following their culture's mode of worship of a god or goddess. When checked later, the strata of society, education or wealth of the life being described often matches authentic descriptions of a person's life from that culture and time.

Often, after a session, clients discover more about the deity mentioned, and excitedly send me confirmation of these validations. Those are cases where the conscious mind knew nothing about the topic, making it more authentic. When clients say they were famous it's best to explore their answers to your questions from many angles, and discover what the relevance of those details mean to the present personality.

Past Life Characters

When accessing another character or past life experience, have the client fully integrate their consciousness with that body and share with you the impressions received. Ask questions such as: "What do you feel like? What is your body like? What are you wearing? What are you thinking?" These questions can be interspersed with deep breathing by saying: "Take a deep breath and as you exhale (ask the questions you want answered)." This is the easiest way for analytical types who think they should be 'doing something', when you really want them to feel through their awareness and through the body, and not think with the mind as the feelings are more authentic. At times it may be that they are observing the character and watching things from a distance as the story unfolds. Having them merge their consciousness with that past life personality, to sense what they feel and think, will usually bring the client into character. Merging consciousness is another form of telepathy, in which we access the thoughts and feelings of another. In shamanic terms, this is known as 'entering the landscape of another.'

Quite frequently becoming some form of energy is experienced, rather than a human form. As with all experiences it is important to have the client integrate their awareness into whatever they perceive, through their feelings and impressions. This is an important time to deepen the experience to prevent the conscious mind from intruding, with thoughts that the session isn't working or that they must be making it up. Preventing this from happening is why you let the client know during the pre-talk that these types of experiences may occur. Remember, that unlike dreaming when the CM isn't aware, it is now somewhere in the background observing and will have its own dialogue. Remind clients to let that happen, but pay no attention to it and save any analysis for later when they have gathered all of the information.

A session story:
Learning Within the Soul Group

John, a young man in his twenties, was desperate to escape his life as he worried about nearly everything. One of his phobias included a fear of contracting cancer, and physically he had problems in the stomach area. To stop his verbal flow I asked him to close his eyes when speaking about his fears, and tell me where he could feel anything in his body. In a way this is a marker to show where healing needs to occur, and it helps the client to deepen their 'yes' mind-set. When speaking about these things we reinforce the connection to surface in our unconscious mind. This is all a part of the induction and deepener, and I watched as he began to nod in agreement with me. I wrote two significant words during the pre-talk: trust and injustice.

The session begins with him standing on soil as a man looking at his feet, which are 'fat and ugly.' He feels he is a guardian of the community. Moving ahead, he finds himself looking down at a waterfall, wanting to escape. He knows something is wrong and thinks of his people, but he will betray them if he jumps. He thinks of going back but doesn't know what to do as he will be slaughtered by invaders from nearby villages. He should have been guarding the place but he didn't see them coming, now it's too late and life isn't worth living as he will be alone. As he runs away, he feels shame at letting the others down and sees flames coming from the village and knows it's all over. Although scared, he returns to the village and hides behind trees. The invaders then comb through the forest looking for survivors and find him. After being beaten he has a sword run through his stomach and he lies there passively.

I ask what decisions or thoughts he is having five minutes before he leaves his body, and he answers: "Nobody will remember him, his life was a waste, he failed people, he wasn't as strong as he was supposed to be." There are many regrets. He also adds that there is sadness in not having someone to cry for him, because he was ugly and never loved. He was also used to doing the hard work and was taken advantage of.

Looking back, after leaving the body he is glad it's over. He looks over the village and then, after seeing it on fire, wants to leave. He is "both happy and sad" for wasting his life there and he decides to go. On the other side he is scared as he's on his own, so he looks up and waits, and then floats, saying: "I know where I'm going…what's happening…and it's overwhelming."

He moves up and sees that "Earth is becoming smaller and smaller." Someone is moving towards him with a group that he can't see very clearly. A female is waving her hands, calling him to her. She is expecting him, she doesn't look at him but he knows she is there for him. Then she takes his hand and they walk together like a "married couple going down the aisle", and not only can he see both of them from behind, but he can feel himself walking by her. He finds this extra-perception normal, but odd. (When not confined to the body there is a 360-degree sensory awareness.)

She takes him to meet with a group of people, and I ask if this is his soul group but he is unsure, saying: "I am a new member." The group members all have different personalities but love each other, and have decided to stay as a group to learn. "I feel I am a new member that doesn't like discipline, I don't like to be told what to do and I go against things," he says. "Generally in life, when the group decides together, I want to have my own opinion and do what I want." He discovers that he spent too much time recovering from something, "like a healing process that took ages and I was in isolation."

I wonder whether they can show him that history or if he can revisit it in some way: "I feel that I was alone, I had to be there...with visitors from time to time. I had to rebalance my energy, as it was broken from fighting all the time and being a bad person." I ask if he can see any of this or be shown any of it: "I see fire, and chains similar to what slaves wore on their wrists and ankles, and vile things." This is his history that is being shown, so we don't need to visit any specific lifetime.

"I am always chasing or being chased by people, so I had to stay in the healing environment to find myself again, then reconnect and rejoin the group so that is why I feel new. It is my group but I haven't been with them for a long time." He is told: "Not to worry, someone had to do it and it's part of what we do. The group is learning about moving by grace, being taught, having to learn how to do things, to interact with each other and other groups."

"This is what we do; we just learn things. To learn how to help people and to redeem myself of the things I did, to be compassionate and help people understand this is just a journey. To help them realise that life is not what it seems to be. And if we want to be together forever as a soul group we can…and life is not really important. It's all experiences and it's like a game. After I came back from my healing I spoke about my experiences and healing, but they said I had to go back and prove myself. A part of me is here always watching me, sometimes not very happily, and sometimes he tries to speak to me and I know it's him and I just block my ears. Sometimes even, when I am listening I think it's my imagination."

I ask if he is aware of his higher self being present. "I can see him, he is right here, and he doesn't look arrogant but I don't know if I want to meet him." So I wonder if his group would think it beneficial for him to meet his higher self if he chose to meet with him. He receives the encouragement to do so.

His higher self says: "In a way he doesn't want to get too involved with my life and he says to me, 'But you already know, why do you want to know more?' He then describes the scene as everyone gathers around to watch this interaction between him and his higher self, who is sitting in the centre. They are curious to know why his higher self is not looking at my client, who is trying to make all kinds of gestures to make face and eye contact. He sees now that they don't have the same face.

His higher self "…is bright, like the sun is all over his face radiating light really brightly." His higher self now looks at him, takes his hand and pulls him closer. "His palm is huge in comparison, my hand is darker than his, it's like my hand disappears in the light and is in a mist of warmth, love, security and bliss." I have him breathe in all of this feeling at a deep cellular level and watch him sink deeper down into trance.

His higher self tells him he loves him but he is to learn how to love himself more, he has to do it, and that if he does this then his higher self can love him even more. "Love is always there but I have to be able to see it and not block it, and I must connect with it, but love that comes from him. I broke the communication with him, just like unplugging a cable. He says he communicates with me but it is me who doesn't want to see this, as though I don't believe. His higher self says he was a bit distant at first, because…he wasn't really disappointed but I really could do better, but it is ok…not in a judgmental way though. It is complicated because I feel like he knows what I am doing now, and he says he and everyone else is pleased. There is no bad, it is all good and I have been hard on myself sometimes."

The purpose with all the vile lives was that: "I wasn't supposed to have all of those, but in some lives I took pleasure in having control of all those people, and my higher self says that's OK but there was another lesson. I also did have some good lives. The lesson when I was killed was; even if you haven't got a family there are other people who can care for you and love you. You must be grateful for those things and give back the love you receive. Don't feel sorry for yourself, be who you are, what you are, and be happy within yourself.

"It's my fault that I couldn't see my higher self earlier in my life, and it's all fear." I ask if he can see examples of times that his higher self showed itself, and he describes: "When I'm about to do something that I shouldn't be doing, he is always there saying (he does this in a deep firm voice) 'Don't do it.' I never think it is coming from him, I think it is just my conscience, but my higher self communicates through my conscience." The higher self then gives him a physical sensation, "similar to the vibrations I feel when I meditate. It is a sign from him that he is always there for me…also during the day when I get those vibrations it is him." He now gets his presence felt as: "A tingling in my right side like a pulsation."

It seems now that it would be a good time to speak with his SC, and it demonstrates the connection and balancing of karma: "He is learning he is important, which he needs to know as he thought he was worthless, he has a conflict between feeling important but taken advantage of. Learn to believe in yourself, be strong and care about yourself more. Caring for others is good but he should also care for himself. He can begin by stopping being so emotional and detaching from any negativity around him. Be conscious of how he is caring and why. Learn to cope when he sees others around who are less fortunate, and appreciate what he has. He could become more aware and strong, and stop wasting energy trying to please others. Instead he can focus within, on himself."

The SC commented on his darker lives: "He was in control for a long time and did bad things, and in a way now its time for him to find peace. He learned every time he was visiting with his group, and had big talks with them about what he did. In a way it was a learning game, but now it's over. He learned through the negative things that you don't find love, and when you don't find love you are alone, and then his soul cannot move forward. He needs to realise how happy he is already – he is happy but thinks about negative things. He needs to stop and see that life is good. He could prioritise, find motivation, and focus attention on more positive things, like coming here today to communicate with me. He needs to meditate, but is lazy. He needs to open up to people and be more honest with his feelings. When he is happy he is to say it, and the same when he is sad. Stop worrying, we have a plan and can only interfere so much into other people's choices.

"The worry is from not protecting the village, as he felt not good enough to protect them and he let them down, so now feels he wants to be there for everybody. Having seen that connection he can forgive himself for everything, relax and let it go. We (the SC) don't need to forgive him, as nothing is wrong or right. He needs to stop trying to redeem himself, as there is nothing to redeem. He is to learn through love." I am told that although his emotional pain is all gone, the sword has left behind certain issues with his abdomen. This receives light and healing which he describes in detail how "it removes all the negativity that was left behind." All was forgiven: "His abdomen has issues that go around his body, and if we heal that it will heal everything."

He learns he is to be a guide for his sister now in this life, and that it will be practice and preparation for becoming a guide on the other side with his group work when he returns.

CHAPTER 9

INTERWEAVING WITH THE NONPHYSICAL

Seeing Blackness, Darkness or Nothing

SOMETIMES THE FIRST session is for the client's subconscious to discover if they can trust you, and when they discover they can, they allow themselves to go deeper into trance in later sessions. This sense of security allows the conscious mind to release the need to keep them safe and protected from the unknown. I have often found that when there is fear and uncertainty, and the client often finds themselves surrounded by blackness, it could be they have gone into what shamanism describes as the lower world, or their subconscious lower mind that is connected to the shadow self. This can be scary, as it is a place of fear, self-avoidance or rejection.

Sometimes when switching from the outer to the inner senses, the client may feel that they are seeing nothing. Don't worry—stay calm, soothing and supportive in tone and manner. Don't apply pressure or cause the client tension. Just help them explore this place with their feelings, not their mind. Do everything you can to eliminate thinking, which triggers conscious mind activity. The goal is to become creative in assisting them to expand their consciousness through sensing and feeling all their inner senses and to creating movement. If needed you can let them know that they can always return to this place later on, to gather more information if they wish.

Seeing nothing could be due to many reasons that may initially elude us, for example, it may be that the client was blind in a past life they are accessing, or they may have died and left the body. It is helpful if they ask for a guide, helper or someone that can help them when they are in such a space. Guiding them to send out telepathically (silently, by thought) a request for their higher self to send help will usually bring a quick response. The help might not be a person, but a thing, or a move into another experience. Another option may be to guide them to move to a significant moment from wherever they are. Movement can go in any direction. Explore whatever led up to being in that particular scene or awareness, or what occurs after that.

There are times when the impressions or imagery are surreal and the client can find no way to express this in words. That's fine, encourage them to do their best, to accept and report all impressions without editing them.

When interacting with some multidimensional energy, the imagery may seem quite unusual in feel or texture. The images may even be holographic in nature, which can be puzzling as the client processes how things appear. When they listen to their recording later, they will access the same states of consciousness and be able to retrieve additional information that was not spoken about during the session.

Entering Dimensions or Other Realities

As our awareness expands inward, descriptions of energy opportunities for movement and travelling such as tunnels, wormholes, spirals or a vortex are often 'seen', and these may open up as entry points into other realms of consciousness. When clients describe these we must ask them what they feel like doing now, for example, do they interact or enter into them, and how do they feel when becoming aware of them? We don't tell them this usually happens to move them through to other dimensions, simply because that may have been the case with other people, but may not be true for them. Instead we must discover how they feel and what they choose to do. If they exhibit any fears those must be explored first, then perhaps move them forward. In a worst-case scenario ask if they would like their higher self to accompany them. If so, suggest they telepathically send a message out for that to take place, and have them describe what happens next. They can also reconnect at any time to the sun imagery (from the previously mentioned diagram) to gather support from their soul, or other members of their soul group.

Working through the Abstract and Colours

The hypnotherapy session involves communication using the same parts of the creative mind that we use when dreaming. When experiencing hypnosis, the client may feel and sense things that may or may not seem familiar, but it is best for them to suspend any judgments and simply share the first things that come into awareness, without editing or attempting to analyse any of the information.

It's best to approach each session as though it is a blank canvas, so that there are no expectations about why or what will unfold. The meaning will be revealed directly to the client at the appropriate time and in a way for them to understand why. As consciousness expands, and the finer realms become more accessible to a growing portion of the population, first-hand experiential knowledge of these realms are becoming more commonplace. A great deal of sensory phenomena that used to be thought of as paranormal has now shifted position into the mainstream, and is considered to be normal. The human mind is now able to perceive, absorb, interpret and communicate with more raw data and abstract information than ever before. When we shift our awareness inward into the more subtle realms, we discover colours, sounds and other sensory stimulus that interacts with our consciousness in very real ways. In many cases, such phenomena will actually communicate and dialogue with us in very normal but telepathic ways.

A radio can be tuned to different frequencies, which is similar to how consciousness can be tuned into through different wavelengths or frequencies. Awareness however, travels far beyond the scope of radio waves, as it includes the clarity and amplification of all senses, including visual and emotive experiences. When listening to the radio or observing a TV programme, we experience only what we are aware of. Guided visualisations imitate daydreaming and activate the right brain. Hypnosis, however, stimulates both left and right hemispheres.

Questions like the following can open up communication and move the session forward, while also deepening the trance state as the focus of the client shifts more deeply inward. When it comes to non-physical things or even other life forms we can ask: "Is it aware of you? Is there something it wants you to know or see?" or "Is there somewhere it wants to take you?" Such questions create movement to take the client deeper into the experience and into trance, which enables them to experience all of creation as alive and conscious. You could add: "What is it trying to convey to you? Take a deep, slow breath and simply allow everything to become more clear, and tell me what you are now aware of." I always use the deep breath and exhalation as a mode of shifting awareness as I've earlier embedded the suggestion that each exhalation will deepen the trance state. I also ask: "Can you send out the question as a thought-like telepathy, to ask if it is connected with or to you in some way? The colours, sounds etc., are vibrational frequencies, so just allow them to do whatever they need to do to help you. "Are you near the colours, inside them, or around them? Just ask the colours to do whatever they need to do to create a healing response in your body, mind and spirit, and describe to me what happens next," or "Send out the thought for the colours to give your body a physical sensation. Can you ask them to increase the feeling level so that you are very sure of receiving it, and tell me what happens now?" Other questions could include: "Can you ask the colours, sounds etc. to work with other areas of your body that might need balancing or healing? And while that is happening, can you ask the colours for whatever else is needed? Can you allow yourself to become even more receptive to this? What else are you noticing now within your body?" or "What else has come into your awareness?"

Colours will sometimes change or mutate into beings, sounds can become healing vibrations that are felt very deeply within the body, and various tones of all kinds will often take the client into higher vibrational levels of experience that can lead to interactions with other beings, planets and star systems. There have been innumerable kinds of phenomena described, as people access and explore the SC or super-conscious realms. Sometimes, just when you think you've heard it all, new and even more thought-provoking concepts get presented, which transcend both cultural and personal beliefs and differences. Colour and light therapies are used effectively to cure many diseases and disorders, so we should not be afraid of working with those aspects of consciousness during our sessions.

A Session Facilitated Only by Colours

This whole session was conducted by colours. The colours interacted with the client, worked on his body and answered questions. The colour spectrum can be measured as vibrational frequencies and can convey information or interact in the consciousness fields. If they show up in a prominent way, we must find out why, or at least not dismiss their value lightly.

Vince's session began with "fractal of colours" behind his eyelids, and evolved into a light show that interacted with his body even causing body sensations in places where he needed healing. When I asked questions, he would tell me what the colour or colours were communicating to him. His SC later expressed the reasons for the color sensory interactions were because he is too attached to his thinking, he needed to feel, be fully into his body awareness, and appreciate his body.

The examples below were the type of questions I asked, to develop movement and dialogue:

(C) is the client (L) is myself

L. OK, you don't have to see anything else besides the colors, just tell me what you sense about it or them. What does it want you to know? Take a deep slow breath and allow everything to become clearer and tell me what you are aware of. (I always use the deep breath/exhalation as I've already embedded the notion to them that each deep breath deepens their trance.) Can you send out the thought (shifting the mind into using telepathy) to ask if it (they) is connected to or with you? Now tell me what you notice.

Some of the things he said:

C. I feel warmth coming from inside of it, I'm seeing blue and pink. I feel like green things folding up. I'm trying to make images happen from the colours I'm getting.

L: Don't try, just let things happen.

C. There are the most beautiful visuals in front of me.

L. OK...just breathe in those most beautiful visuals and describe any one of them that you want to.

C. Sort of spots, different colours moving toward me... silver spots moving toward me like a tunnel and I'm trying to decide if I want to go through the tunnel.

L. OK make a decision and if it is yes find yourself moving through the tunnel and see where it takes you.

C. They are changing colours.

L. Mmmhh and what colours are there?

C. Mauve, dark purple, grey, green, indigo.

L. It sounds quite beautiful.

C. The colours are changing and moving towards, me... very strong colours, not actual forms though.

L. The colours are frequencies so just let them do whatever they need to...are you near the colours, or in or around them?

C. I'm in them.

L. Just ask the colours to do whatever they need to... .whatever healing is needed, for your mind, your body or your spirit, and tell me what happens next.

C. *They are moving in waves now, down, towards me.*

L. *Excellent, just send out the thought for the colours to connect somehow with your body and give your body a sensation of the work being done and where it is taking place.*

C. *I'm travelling down some orangey cloudy wispy...*

L. *When you say travelling down what do you mean?*

C. *Some cloudy wispy colours... sort of floating towards me.*

L. *Does it connect with your body?*

C. *I can feel it in my hands and my hands are tingling, they have been tingling from the start. I can feel the visuals inside me connecting with my hands.*

L. *Can you ask them to increase the feeling in your hands so that you're very sure of this, and tell me what happens next?*

(He confirms that this has increased a few times.)

L. *Can you ask the colours to work with other areas of your body that might need some balancing or healing?*

C. *My feet now have the same feeling as in my hands.*

L.: *... while that's going on can you ask for whatever else is needed that the colours can do, and tell me what else you notice in your body?*

C. *Whatever it is, there is some slight pains in my chest around my heart.*

L. *Can you ask the colour to help you in the very best way and if it is working around your heart, can you ask the colours to ripple the feeling throughout your body so that you can become the very best that you can?*

C. *I see a black thing floating away, like a mist.*

L. *It's floating away from your heart?*

C. *(He laughs quite happily.) Yes, it's floating away*

from my heart.
   L. Mmmhhh and what else is happening now?

Abreactions

Sometimes during hypnosis the client may have deep emotional purgings or a release of repressed emotional memories known as an abreaction.

Abreactions are a natural hypnosis phenomena albeit an uncommon one. The SC will use any opportunity to create equilibrium within the body. Often deep relaxation and an opening of the expanded energy fields will release these emotional blocks. I've even known this to take place as soon as the client lies down even before the induction, which suggests that the session has been seen as a much needed, powerful release of repressed emotions. There are therapeutic strategies that are primarily focused on the cathartic release of these emotions, however, when working through the guidance of the SC it is not usually necessary to have a severe emotional release besides crying deeply.

When a client has an abreaction it is a simple matter of staying very calm and asking them to open their eyes whilst reassuring them to breath deeply into their body. Have them focus on something in the room or on their breathing as that will engage their left brain while minimising any continued emotional reactions. The key is to bring their awareness back into the present, which will shift them out of their feelings. We cannot act and react at the same time, so we provide them with an 'action.' It is very important that we minimise as much physical contact as possible throughout the whole session as you'll run the risk of anchoring them to the abreaction. A future touch by someone in that same place may release the emotion that was anchored there. Most importantly don't freak out, but do some deep, calm breathing yourself... through resonance your client will calm down by your lead. Only when they have calmed down do you explore what triggered that reaction. Staying calm, confident and authoritative enables the client to feel safe as they will trust your ability as a source of strength and comfort for them.

The ideal is to not bring them out of trance with unreleased emotions and unresolved issues. Having them take a deep breath as they exhale, means they can relocate their special place that makes them feel really good and peaceful. Taking the breath calms them down, distracts them and refocuses them on peace. It might be that they need to spend some time there as you provide them with positive reinforcement while reminding them that they are only reviewing this as they have already survived it.

Intuition

Be open to your intuition; don't think you have to come up with the answers because you don't want to lead. Instead you want to guide your clients to their own discoveries. There is no need to analyse or think about anything that occurs, just stay open and receptive. As practitioners we must believe in the process and in the client, knowing that the SC will reveal what is important. However, without many tools or techniques in our toolbox we limit the quality of the experience. Trusting in the process will mean, at times, that you will have to discard any preconceived idea of how the script should be adhered to, and allow your creativity the freedom of working intuitively with the client. With practice and continued learning we become skilled at obtaining therapeutic results, rather than just addressing the patterns that reveal themselves.

Significant or Important Moments

The SC knows exactly what needs to be brought forward into conscious awareness, why, and how it will help the client achieve their life purpose, or their reasons for existing. The life milestones are shown as significant moments or events and these are important. They should be explored at the feeling, knowing and experiential levels. Significant events may leapfrog into other lifetimes or energy experiences, so just follow the client's lead and allow the SC to direct the flow and the release of information. Some scenes do not require much more investigation than what is perceived at the feeling level, while others are quite detailed and may involve many additional characters, some of whom may be known in the current life, and others who may be recognised as members of a soul group.

If you find things are not moving forward, direct the client to another significant or important moment or event. You can do this at any point throughout the session; no matter what type of life experience is being explored. They can also be directed backwards of forwards in time to revisit any of these later in the session.

Some clients meet up with gender specific soul aspects. Women are meeting a masculine energy that helps them throughout the session, and, when asked what their connection is with the client we are told it is their 'husband' and men are meeting with their 'wife.' Those words always bring laughter or astonishment. Further exploration shows them that this is their own male/female aspect that needed integration with them. When energy or a helping spirit shows up early in the session I do not bother asking what the connection is to the person, but instead have them help the client by showing them things or taking them places according to 'what they want the client to know.' This deepens the trance, initiates an exploration into their consciousness, and prevents the client processing their deeper connection so early into the session. Trust in the willingness of these 'spirits' to assist is built by doing this. These helping spirits can always be called back in at any time throughout the session and invited to show, teach, or explain whatever transpires. In reality, they often are in the background and never far away. Because we are working within quantum realities, we do not need to stick with a particular format as your intuition will guide you on how best to interact.

Patience

Patience is a virtue that all practitioners should aspire to develop, as it underpins all communication. Restraint may be needed to provide the necessary time and space for internal processes to transpire. Watch for physical signs that indicate that the client is relaxing and shifting states of consciousness. When working therapeutically with others, silence can be a great way to allow the client to move through feelings and gain insight that might otherwise escape their awareness. Also, asking too many questions quickly defeats the purpose, as few questions will get answered or create positive responses until the underlying emotion has been acknowledged and processed. Patience and persistence create the supportive framework that will help to ensure a successful session.

Keep the Client Talking

When in a state of relaxed, deep hypnosis, the client often feels perfectly at peace and in a state of a raised holistic vibration. Sometimes, the questions the conscious mind deemed so important beforehand seem mundane and unimportant when viewed from the higher perspective of the SC. Without the practitioner assisting the client and directing their attention back to the questions, revelations and important insights could be glossed over. It is important to keep the client talking, because the recording of the session may be their only memory, especially when working with somnambulistic clients.

Hypnotic impressions can fade as quickly as a dream fades from the waking mind. Just as in dreams, our subconscious uses images and storylines that feel real while we are experiencing them, and are filled with meaning and insight as we analyse them later. Therefore, the more we experience, the larger our potential for growth and release. It is our job to get the client's questions answered by the client's own SC while they are in trance. When the questions are answered they are usually a clear response to what is asked, yet much more information is potentially available.

It is best to approach whatever is said from a sceptical perspective, as this allows us to be more thorough in our questioning and gathering of details. We are more likely to get the best results when we approach our questioning from a variety of angles — without prejudice or assumption — which results in more clarity for both client and practitioner. How many ways can you ask the same question? How often can you go back to the same point smoothly and effortlessly? How easily can you transition from one subject to another?

The depth of hypnosis can be so peaceful and nourishing that just hearing someone speaking to you and asking questions can feel like an intrusion or seem annoying, so as practitioners we must maintain the fine balance between our communications, the client's responses, and the client's continued relaxation.

Never Lead

Ideally we need to draw out more of the client's own perceptions and self-awareness. What do they think, feel, experience, and what are they aware of in each moment? If we ask leading questions we don't end up with authentic material, because we haven't allowed information to flow naturally through the client, untainted by the practitioner. When working with the SC you don't want a compliant client who thinks they need to please you—ideally you want a client who speaks freely about their experience. Leading is never allowed, as the practitioner can lead the mind into creating false memories.

Angels, Helpers, Guides and Healers

Angels, guides, or highly evolved energies can be called upon at any time to help the client, especially when it comes to any form of healing. I often wonder if those who show up as angels are really the client's higher self, spirit guides, soul friends or helpers, as consciousness often presents itself in whatever kind of form will best help the client. Sometimes they show themselves as those mythological characters with whom the client feels a cultural, spiritual or religious connection. Angels are healing energies that often assist with soul integration, reclaiming fragments, and with the release of ideas or beliefs that the client may be holding onto that actually belong to someone else. Healing such reclaimed or released parts should always be done with divine unconditional love and light, which the angels also use.

These beings are often described as transparent light with differing shades and hues, and are associated with the higher self. These colours may be experienced as translucent, or like the shifting rainbow illusion of an incandescent mother of pearl. An orb shape is one of the most frequently described forms used when people describe themselves as energy, and they use terms like a globe of light, a bubble or a ball.

Often during quantum-oriented sessions a client accesses the afterlife. Depending on the questions asked, this can become a passing reference point or we can specifically explore this in-depth. It is a good idea to explore this inter-life state when the client wants to learn more about themselves as this is where they connect to their soul essence. When these opportunities arise with my clients I explore them thoroughly as there is much to be gained. From here, we can access aspects that are relevant to the person, their immediate inquiries and then receive information suitable to the individual's level of conscious awareness. That becomes obvious with the quality and variety of the information provided, for example, is the information revealed personal or empirical in nature? Is it simplified or complex? Does it apply to everyone universally?

Sometimes the information is tainted by the conscious mind of the client, confirming that our personal beliefs can intrude and prevent direct communication from a higher perspective, especially when there is an emotional investment in not changing or healing. Whatever level of consciousness comes through, however, is in some way connected to the client. It is best, therefore, to aim for the highest quality of wisdom possible.

We cannot force a person to access higher information than their soul brings forward, and any self-doubt will only lower the vibration of the session. We can, however, creatively negotiate the foundation necessary for a raised vibrational frequency.

Sometimes facilitating a session in a very dense energy space can also affect the quality of a session, giving rise to thoughts about the external intrusion on the quality of material available. Since there is a collaboration of energy or vibrational frequencies involved when we co-create with others, the space can affect the depth and height of information available.

The quality of the information may be expressed as monosyllabic and cryptic, and at other times expressed in a non-stop verbal flow, which is sometimes humorous or detached and serious. With such variety, can we really say it is the same quality, consistency or level of mind communicating with or through each individual? The SC only provides the information that is suitable for the client's understanding, as anything else would confuse the client and lower their vibration. The ultimate goal is to increase one's vibration, not lower it.

Healing Cellular Memories

When treating physical problems sometimes feelings surface that also need to be healed. For example, when treating the liver it can bring up feelings of anger that is stored there. These are passing feelings exiting as they are releasing the condensed energy blocks that were created by the original cause. As those specific areas of the body heal there is no place for anything but good health with energy flowing through and around the organs. Any area of the body can store memories from a time, a place or a situation which gets activated in times of stress. Some of this impacts on our neurological system and has been carried through from the soul's history into the current lifetime for resolution, healing or understanding.

It could also be that memories needs to come up for conscious recognition to release it permanently without anything else needing to be done. However the client won't know this until their subconscious reveals the significance. The reasons are not always generic or predictable, but will always have a themed story that will be insightful. Anything that lowers the consciousness will trigger things held in the weakest areas of the body, and if it's in the cells it will come up when given the opportunity.

I have found it to be tremendously important in our work to have the body cells release trapped memories and trauma. Our cells are surrounded by water and our body is largely water and water holds memories... you can have the cells release anything that is no longer needed, such as memories, pain, emotions, toxins, etc.

If pain has been felt during the healing then it is important that time is spent to complete the healing process of eliminating any painful feelings. An agreement can be made with the SC that healing continues over the next days, weeks or however long it takes, as well as their inspiring the client intuitively to do things that supports any healing undertaken, and create life-affirming decisions daily.

The Afterlife:
The Death Transition

The day of death — as the spirit transitions away from the body — and the next phase of the experience are crucial consciousness moments for the soul. What will that life just re-experienced mean to the other aspects of self? Which belief systems are being retained and which are being released?

Time should be spent exploring the last day of a life. Those feelings, decisions and beliefs will have to be processed and released to clear any residual energy. After death, when the soul is free, an energy clearing is often described as taking place before they move on or further inwards. In such cases shift the client back to events leading up to that last day or to another significant moment before that day. Only after such exploration is made should you move them forward to the arrival scene or interlife experience.

With brutal or painful deaths the soul generally exits

the body before the actual death occurs, watching the body from afar as it dies. Some feel so deeply called to be free of the body that they exit quickly, without experiencing any lingering concern or curiosity about the body's actual death. They detach from the death scene instantly and express no interest in finding out what happened to the body after it expired. Even so, it is still important to explore the last day of life and how the consciousness was preparing for transition.

Not all clients report seeing a light, float upwards, or become aware of other beings at death. Sometimes they say: "There is nothing," and when asked what is happening now, they don't know what they are to do next. Rarely, although it does occasionally happen, they say that they need to find another body. This should be explored for a variety of reasons and may lead to a need for soul integration. Are they going to reincarnate immediately? Are they going to stay within the earth vibration and/or attach to someone else? What exactly do they mean by that comment? Refocus them on the life they have just exited, explore how they felt about that lifetime and what their thoughts are now they have left that body. Afterlife perceptions always differ from what was experienced in the body.

After they have left the body some souls choose to stay around their home or community; most are pleased to be free and float away, while others choose to have a look at something local to them. To do this, they float away but do not remark on their ability to do so as they accept it as completely natural. Those who die with strong feelings of anger or frustration may still be attached to the story and cannot move on without help. Rarely has a soul told me during a session that they will become a ghost so that they can get back at someone but it may occur, which will lead to a need to process and release that fragmentation. Being able to process unresolved feelings by exploring how they feel and what they might have done differently helps to prevent fragmentation or attachment to others.

One client saw herself in a past life starving in her little home in the woods. It was wintertime and she had gone out to see if she could find some food, only to collapse. As she lay there freezing, she floated away into the light and met with her deceased daughter and husband. Thinking she had died, I was surprised to discover that in her next significant moment she was lying in her bed, sick and chilled, but had survived her ordeal. She had experienced a near death experience (NDE), but not a permanent transition. This is a clear example of why we must not make assumptions, or attempt to lead the client anywhere to suit our ideas or assumptions about what might happen next.

The Life Planning Stages

If this is an area that the client wants to explore they can be guided back to the planning stages of how and why decisions were made prior to coming into life. Do not expect that they will immediately meet with their committee as it may be that they return to something quite abstract, such as an energy state, a colour, an alien life form, or anything else that relates to becoming a human on Earth. Explore everything while moving them through the background of why they have been born.

Meeting with the Deceased

The inner realities are the same places accessed through any technique of consciousness exploration or dreams, so it's not surprising that we meet up with those we once knew in our physical lives. Sometimes these individuals become our guides, helpers and soul friends—or they may be stuck and unable to move further inward to their light, or perhaps they have come to relay a message. When they can't move on they stay in the form-based lower astral worlds, and often don't know what to do once they've left the body. If they are stranded we can help direct them to the light of their own source. As a facilitator there is no need to know where they are to go except towards their light.

Healing helpers or angels that may be cleverly disguised as guides or helpers can be called upon to help discarnate spirits move on. This process is usually described by them as 'floating away and becoming light,' when they move into the less-dense, vibrational fields.

The deceased may not always show up in an interactive way, but will sometimes appear as an image. An example of this was with a young man who, immediately on entering trance, saw his mother's image with a still face, and she was unable to communicate with him. As the session progressed it transpired that there was unfinished business. After exploring, clearing, healing and resolving issues that involved her, he saw her image again at the end of the session but this time she was smiling at him. He then felt and saw energy flowing from her chest to his—he described this as pressure in his chest and then his heart expanding.

Another example is a woman who met up with her grandmother as she went into trance. She became very emotional, burst into tears and had a conversation with her. The grandmother said it was OK that she had not gone to see her before she died or attended the funeral—none of these concerns had been mentioned in the pre-talk.

My favourite example was with a woman who spoke only about two middle-aged children, yet on entering trance met with a guide who took her to see her deceased son who spent the entire session with her and they shared quite an adventure. She later said that she never speaks about him as he died a long time ago in his teens. He told her that he is a guide for his brother and sister, and he shared additional personal information that she would not have had any way of knowing.

If the deceased show up we must help the client discover why, and how to make the most of the meeting. We can also help to enhance the love bonds by having them send and receive tangible feelings of love between one another—such feelings can be felt profoundly by the body during hypnosis.

Not Wanting to Come Back

In a few rare circumstances, no matter what is uncovered and experienced, the client may not want to leave their friends or love companions that they meet or unite with in the spirit planes. Some people have yearned for their real home since childhood and feel they don't belong on Earth. Reconnecting with their groups, multidimensional peers or higher self, and receiving pure, unconditional love for what may be the first time in their life, can generate a sense of sadness that lingers for days after the session has ended.

I thought it interesting to show a few examples of entering into the afterlife. There have literally been dozens at least but I've picked these three quite different examples to use. I've tried to stay verbatim to their words but have condensed it for easier reading and length.

1) This person died after having lived with her extended family after her parents had died. She escaped them by marrying at 17 and felt 'liberated' but went on to live a quiet life. The last day of her life found her a woman in her 60s having had a contented life. She feels quite happy having thoughts of leaving this Earth in peace having had a better life than some other people. The last hours' thoughts show her that her only child—a daughter—is single and is going to feel lonely. She decides to leave when she is not looking. She leaves having made a conscious choice to leave. Five minutes before leaving she has a perception of a gateway into a tunnel—like a path opening up in her room that she can just climb into. She floats into it alone (it's a different space in her room that has a different energy to the room so that she can just float into it). She looks back at her body, which is old, and wishes that she could have been more open minded and wants to take more memories of things she knows into her next life. These type of things are about life and 'other worldly' life things but she doesn't know what she means by that. She could have been more loving towards her husband. Her decisions that affect her current life are that she shouldn't be so reserved and to get out more.

Now she leaves the body behind and is really excited about where she is going... it is back home and she knows automatically where it is she is going and how to get there. Now at home, there are lots of people around her that she knows and has missed. They spend time together talking about where they've all been. They are light beings, not in fully human form, with white light around them and yellows and pinks. She's now not a physical body but has a blue hue to her. There is a lot of exchanging of ideas with lots of laughter and humour with what everyone has been through and a bit of sadness as everyone does get a bit attached to their lives (on Earth, in her case).

After spending time with her friends there she tells me that "we actually don't know really what lives we've each have had or the others have led until we ask. It's not like they instinctively know or are told in advance about where everybody is going. We go our separate ways and then meet back in this place, and then we have to reenergise. We sit or be around this stone thing in the middle (of a space) that has a spiral like a vortex of energy coming up from the floor and around it, and we get energised by being near it and it makes us feel a lot better as it's quite a traumatic journey coming back. The energising feels really good and warm all over me and I can feel it in my head, it's like you need it in order for you to connect back to Source. It renews, restores and re-energises our thoughts. After we spend time in this area, which is a meeting or holding place for people. We can stay as long as we like. In this particular place it's for my group but there are others for other groups. But then we can travel off to wherever we want to go."

2) This particular client had just experienced quite a traumatic death where his life was taken prematurely through an execution from a wrongful accusation. He is brutalised, mocked, starved and isolated so there is tremendous emotional charge in this for him prior to his leaving this reality. His decision is to internalise these things and not show any of this on the outside so his energy fields is quite congested with fearful resignation. On his transition to the 'other side' he moves toward a light that he sees and on sending out the thought for someone to greet him, angels appear and he is being hugged. They know him well but will not permit him to ask questions as they are pulling him along in a gliding fashion and they tell him he'll be OK and not to worry. Although he is sad he is feeling trusting of them and loved. They take him to a lighter place that is warmer and they are tending to him by touching him softly and soothing him. He asks where he is and they tell him that

he is safe. The place is a place of healing, which is important they tell him as he is still in shock. They tell him not to ask questions but just to be as they continuously surround him, touching his shoulders, back and head and though he feels better he is lost in his thoughts of those loved ones he's left behind. No matter how they reassure him, his sense of duty to them is painful. They begin moving again to a spa-like place with columns and harps playing. Other people are there who are also laying down and receiving healing. He is told once again, no questions…just heal. (The questions are primarily mine as I try to discover what is taking place and why.) His body is shaking, feeling different and becoming something else as his whole body vibrates, a familiar but different feeling. The fear recedes and it is vibrating fast and deep, outside of his control. The angels are still there overseeing him. Translucent blues, purples, and white light surrounds him, shimmering, and he feels different and can only see himself as light with no real form. He is being transformed and comforted. The transformation is preparing for the next step. He is told to be patient when we ask what this next step is, as the vibrations continue. (No matter how I try I cannot rush this process.) He himself is glowing a variety of colours and he shimmers. When this process is complete he is now moving through the stars with his soul friends/family who he belongs with, and they are taking him on a journey someplace. The session continues in a wonderful way that is not relevant to this discussion.

3) This client has just died in a life that was somewhat mundane, she raised other people's children but had none of her own and felt she died of an ovarian problem in her 40s just when she was beginning to enjoy her husband's new found wealth. She was unable to marry her first love because of responsibilities to her siblings after their mother's death. Her last day decisions were that her life was not one she would have chosen, but decides to look on the positive side of things. She slips out of her body quite easily and thinks it's nice that they'll miss her but is happy to be gone from the pain and discomfort. She feels a lightness of being and that it's fun to be free; she discovers her ability to fly around and a few memories come to mind but nothing that hinders her. As she now moves away from where she lived, she expands her viewpoint of the world/Earth and goes and takes a look. She is then aware that someone has come to see her. He tells her she's had enough time exploring and he laughingly states that she has to come on. It's a big being who feels male and is, in fact, her Higher Self ('I'm you') — she describes an ethereal-type big presence who gently brings her along. They go up as a feeling more like a fast escalator and she is told it's her perception of moving this way, and she is once again 'born again' and being taken to a place of rest. He tells her to stay there for a while to adjust because she had been sick and needs now to be restored.

Entities and the Shadow Side

Shadow people, or 'dark' entities, are a phenomenon of sleep paralysis when our psyche is in an altered state and not fully anchored to the physical body. Also, lucid dreaming is another state of consciousness where we might run across dark beings and entities.

Shamans and others that manoeuvre in the worlds of the altered state speak of such things that we encounter involuntarily in nightmares. Tibetan dream yoga teaches that these manifestations are an image of our own deep unconscious fears. Buddhism also teaches and prepares individuals for what to do when they die, as well as having post-death rituals for the dead to help them move on into the clear light.

However, evidence abounds of lost souls or earthbound spirits who haven't realised they have died. An example of this would be if a person is crossing the road on their way to the shops and is hit by a car, which kills them instantly and knocks the spirit out of the body. Not realising they have died, they continue shopping but can't understand why nobody pays any attention to them. This lack of understanding leads them to become stuck and confused. Such earthbound souls are often rescued by mediums, OBE practitioners and other consciousness explorers; the Lifeline Program at The Monroe Institute has a long history of scientific research in this area.

As fascinating as this research is, earthbound spirits rarely show up in a session, and if such a lost soul does they could be a stuck loved one, a relative of the experiencer or a complete stranger. In such cases it's a matter of helping them move on into the light.

Most often, what is experienced as a 'dark' entity is a rejected part of the psyche that seems to have a life of its own. In rare times — when it is a fearful representation that seems foreign to the client — then exploring when it became attached, and why it has been affecting the client, is recommended, as well as its integration or permanent release. It is interesting to witness first-hand how our fears can take on a life of their own, burying themselves deeply within our subconscious mind to protect us from our own reality. I often tell clients that our subconscious has the job of protecting us from things that we think will overwhelm us. Burying aspects of ourselves causes soul loss, as we lose some of our energy that becomes imprisoned. Shame and negative feelings are usually the root feelings beneath this method of self-preservation.

There has been a good deal of research conducted by prominent authors and therapists into psychic attachment. Many cultural beliefs support the attachment concept, including the Chinese 'hungry ghosts,' similar to 'preta' in Sanskrit, meaning a 'departed, deceased or dead person.' Whether we believe that such lost souls exist is not as important as the client's cultural beliefs. Always stay neutral, enter their reality so that you can help them explore whatever resides within their mind.

As we have already covered, what may seem to be a separate entity from the client's perspective may actually be a rejected or fragmented aspect of the client's own psyche. Fragmentation sometimes occurs during or after a traumatic or shocking event. The rare times that an intrusion is an entirely separate being, such as a deceased loved one or a stranger, healing angels can be called in to assist the spirit in returning to the light. In cases that involve a deceased loved one, the client may have subconsciously taken on their illnesses or temperaments. Sensitive souls can do this unconsciously, for example, when they move into a new home where the previous owner had died, but their energetic presence is still there and being felt. We can track any psychosomatic history back to what was going on in the client's life when the problem first began. Ask: "What are the triggers that activate the symptoms? What kind of thoughts are going on in the client's mind when the symptoms are occurring?" Such questions can help reveal meaningful insights.

Intrusions and Attachments

If there is contact with a lost soul, or there are intrusive externally attached energies, then raise the vibrational quality of the session and proceed from there. Remind the client that they are surrounded by white light; the gold light of their soul, and the overseeing protection of their SC. Rejected or suppressed fears can seem to have a life of their own and contribute unknowingly to many other fears. Or there may be some fragmentation of the psyche caused by abuse, accidents or other negative disturbances. Why not raise that client's vibration to its highest level? Why not focus on raising them up rather than concentrating on the lower feelings? They have been immersed with so much discomfort that just identifying that they exist is enough to begin the healing process. What transpires during the session continues the healing. Always aim to communicate with the highest level of consciousness, but recognise that to get to the top we have to go through the lower levels. To get to the higher self, we have to resolve any toxic feelings held within the energy matrix and the physical body.

Cutting Ties

When asked if there is anything attached or affecting them that does not belong to them, one person responded: "Wow! There are hundreds of hooks falling away from me." It really is not important to discover what all of them are, as that could become time consuming. But for your own self-discovery and research it might be interesting to ask them to follow the thread of one to see where it leads.

Vows, Contracts and Agreements

Vows, contracts and agreements can be broken or destroyed when they are no longer necessary or useful; and soul contracts and agreements don't always involve other people. They can include other forms of personal handicaps such as poverty, places, ill health, life themes or life patterns. I clearly remember one client who was breaking his contract with poverty, and when asked if he wanted to destroy any other contracts, went on to describe in astonishment the 'deluge' that were being destroyed. In any instance where there is pain or anything holding a person back from personal joy I ask: "Are there any contracts or agreements associated with this that can or should be broken now?" This works well for emotions like suffering, guilt or anger. I always ask the client if they would like to do something before I do it. Doing so keeps them in the 'yes' mind-set, and in complete accordance with their soul, which is overseeing change and moving forward.

Spiritual or karmic contracts, and agreements with significant emotional players in our lives can be both frustrating and our greatest learning opportunities. If it is determined that a particular agreement can now be broken or dissolved it will enable instant healing, so long as there is understanding of the underlying reason for the original creation of the agreement. It is irresponsible to simply remove or clear entanglements without first confirming with the SC that it is permissible to do so. Therefore, it is always important to find out what the meaning was or is for that particular experience, the history behind its creation, and what the soul had to learn from the experience.

CHAPTER 10

DIALOGUE WITH THE SUBCONSCIOUS

"When engaging in a dialogue with the higher self, we must test any message we receive in the "fires" of the mind's critical discrimination. We must ask: is this advice really wise? Does it really make sense? This is a vital step, for it is clear that any such message can come from a variety of sources, not only from the higher self or from the lower unconscious, but also from many intermediate ones, where wisdom is combined with varying amounts of distortion, unmet needs and desires, unrelated thoughts and emotions. This discussion of discrimination provides a useful place to make a precise theoretical discrimination concerning the way we have been using the term "higher self" in much of this paper. The dialogue with the higher self is not directly with the higher self. Rather it is with one or another element in our superconscious, which itself is activated by the higher self."
—Dialogue with the Higher Self
www.synthesiscenter.org/articles/1153.pdf

Overall, when it comes to the higher mind dialogue I spend time during the pre-talk encouraging them to have confidence and patience with themselves, which is very effective as it allows them to move confidently onwards so that the communication can take place. The groundwork would have already been done to get the subconscious and the conscious mind working as a team, and rather than focusing on deepening the conscious mind, I find it sometimes more productive to allow the subconscious to rise to the level of conscious awareness. Therefore, the client needs to give themselves the permission to use their internal resources without the need to struggle or strain.

Sometimes a client may feel insecure thinking that they are not deep in trance so they 'cannot' have their higher mind speak through or to them. This makes them start processing and engages the left brain or conscious mind. I've discovered that if I give them the options of a dual way of experiencing their higher mind then it provides them with a greater level of freedom and it is 'artfully vague' enough to prevent any resistance. Doing this effectively creates a 'gap' or space for them to adjust internally into, and apply their own perception or understanding of how this works in a much easier way, for example, 'whether I can go deeper or not the higher mind can still come into my awareness without me feeling I must go deeper... or go anywhere other than where I now am.'

I offer them this as an invitation 'to allow' rather than saying 'you must' and so this is less likely to cause any resistance. I often say 'breathe in deeply and slowly... and as you exhale even more slowly you will know (and insert whatever they need to find out, for example where they are)... '

Sometimes when a person needs help an angel will come and assist and even relay messages through the person. In some cases the subject will meet with their Council of Light and have information relayed directly from them. Of course, the same is true for Spirit Guides. It would seem that any subconscious information can be said to be channelled and depending on the person almost anyone can be directed to go anywhere on the inner planes to meet teachers for purposes of dialogue or healing. Also, in some cases there may be discussions of planetary empirical interests or finding information from the akashic records where they often find themselves at a 'library' type setting looking at their own 'book' of life.

Channelled information speaks of the person they are communicating through in the 3rd person and is often empirical in content, very much like how the client's higher conscious mind communicates with the client. With some individuals this dialogue seems to flow like an open tap and with others it is very hesitant, slow or uses very short syllables. The depth and quality of the information varies even with the same person. I have also noticed that some people, when asked a particular question, will first breathe in very deeply and when they commence communicating the information given, pace and tonality are changed. Yet still it is all being presented as their higher mind.

The higher mind dialogue has nothing to do with past lives, and we do not need to explore those first to speak directly with that level of consciousness. A direct communication with the higher mind encompasses any subject matter relevant and appropriate to the needs of the CM. When working with the SC, if it seems resistant I encourage it by suggesting that it created the problem to get the client's attention, and now that it has their full attention in the session they can go ahead and address them in a way that will finally be heard and acknowledged.

The client may perceive a non-physical being that fits into a belief system, such as those of religions and other spiritual practices. They do not, however, speak of twin souls or flames, spiritual hierarchies, aliens coming to rescue humanity, or anything that removes free will or make demands on the client. The beings that communicate with the clients are loving, and often give no advice unless asked for. I have never personally experienced them making demands, being arrogant or causing unease. The communications between the client and helpers are from a personal interactive level, with no names given unless asked for. The response is often that they are friends or helpers and they share unconditional love between all parties.

My friend and fellow practitioner, Joren Kinnetz, quoted below, started asking people how they experienced their awareness of their higher mind directly communicating through them and he found there were three ways that most people responded:

1. The person feels like they just step to the side and allow someone else to speak. They don't feel like they're the one actually speaking.
2. They hear the words 'in their head' and they just repeat them.
3. They see some form of picture or vision and they interpret it.

As Joren Kinnetz states:

"I've found most people fall into category number two or a combination of number two with another type. I myself have been a client twice and found that I usually hear the words and repeat them, but sometimes I'm off to the side as an observer. During my sessions I felt like I was making the responses up because I felt like I was still present. That is until I went back and listened to the recording. That is when I realised how amazing the information coming through was and that was not how I usually talk.

"It's also important during the interview to explain to your client what to expect when the SC is called in. Tell them the three main ways they might experience the SC, and that no matter what thought or idea comes through to just repeat it. It may feel like they're making it up at the moment, but when they go back and listen to the recording, they'll understand that the information was coming from a higher place. Since I started giving this information out in the interview, I can't remember the last time the SC didn't come through for the person."

When it comes to long-term permanent healing of a very serious illness it is not enough to communicate with the SC and have it tell you, "Yes the healing has been done." That simplistic approach does not necessarily mean that it is so. It is much better to cover all bases in order to support the totality of the work, and access higher understanding as to why the illness or discomfort manifested in the first place. What did/does this event represent within the larger context or stream of consciousness? What purpose did it serve for the individual? What kind of life can now be created with this new knowledge and understanding?

For increased success during a session it is important that we help the client create a future foundation for new growth to evolve. We can also support the understanding of their own participation in the process, and offer them support. This process begins during the pre-talk, as questions and comments are shared that require the client to think. This thinking process stimulates a response from the SC during hypnosis as the SC rebalances and harmonises the energy fields to ensure feelings of well being around all subjects discussed. If the client leaves feeling unsure of the efficacy of the session then they could be prone to falling into old habits and patterns.

Diet plays a big role in our feelings and determines the quality of life we can experience. What, if anything, needs to be added to or removed from the diet and why? The SC can give suggestions to increase the vitality of the body and energy field. Being told to eat fruit or vegetables is also a way to receive colour therapy, which in itself maintains a raised vibratory field. Being told to eat yogurt because of a probiotic need is not something we may consciously think about, but the body does not lie and it knows what it needs nutritionally, spiritually and physically. Those with mental problems have been told to omit wheat or gluten from their diets without any previous conscious knowledge about this connection with their challenges, and later discover this to be true and known to the medical profession.

Speaking with the Higher Mind and Parts Therapy

Parts Therapy teaches that we can communicate with areas of the mind that know the reasons and solutions necessary for complete healing. We can ask to speak with the soul, higher self or higher consciousness of a person, or to the parts of them that know the answers or can do the healing. Remember that all the resources we need are within us, and that parts of us reside in various states or levels of consciousness. If you would like more information on Parts Therapy, I recommend you visit:
http://www.royhunter.com/articles/what-is-parts-therapy.htm

> *Amazing insight can come from such parts of ourselves. When such a voice is contacted, a strong empowerment may take place. We are beginning to connect to inner sources of strength and wisdom.*
> —John Rowan: Discover Your Subpersonalities (Routledge, 1993)

Silent Communication

When the client gives permission to allow their SC to communicate with you but then becomes silent, giving no responses to your questions, this can cause you to lose confidence. Firstly, maintain a calm, soothing tempo and pace while paying attention to the non-verbal clues as to what might be taking place within the client. Have they become still? Has the blood flow retreated further away from the surface of their skin? Are the eyelids fluttering (REM)? Are the facial muscles really relaxed? Has the client become tense or restless? These are all good indications of something occuring under the surface that can be worked with creatively. Sometimes they may not give an affirmative response but will repond to your questions through their body language.

Speak to them in the third person tense to shift the mind away from the individuated personality ego or CM, while repeating your questions in various ways after appropriate pauses. If this gets no response then use a deepener to refocus the depth of trance, adding at the end: "Please tell me about the first thing that comes into your awareness now." Be open as to how their responses may come, while acting as though whatever occurs is completely natural and 'textbook' normal. Responses vary — it could be that the client is receiving an intense healing that is being felt in the body, even though they are not communicating this. They may have some degree of memory later on, of what was taking place within them in response to your questions.

Sometimes the client may seem to be in a deep sleep, but then opens their eyes as soon as you finish speaking confirming their awareness of your communication. When they fall 'asleep' you can continue communicating with the SC, and even if you don't get a response the information will still go directly into the subconscious. Sleep-learning is also an effective way to bypass any conscious mind interference or limitations. In fact, it's a rapid way to receive and retain new information. In some cases the visual responses may be abstract rather than a direct verbal communication, like seeing a box with a tick in it to mean yes.

CHAPTER 11

CLOSURE AND EXITING THE SESSION

THERE WILL BE many opportunities for applying closure, beginning with the client's need for having the session. There may be things they want to end, change, reintegrate or complete in their lives. Like all good stories there is a beginning (the pre-talk) the middle (the hypnosis) and the end, which begins before they leave the hypnotic state and continues throughout the post-talk. During hypnosis there is the closure of scenes and instructions for all participating energies to return to their rightful places. This gives the client time and space to make their own internal adjustments, as they return to present day awareness.

Drawing the session to a conclusion makes it necessary to tie up loose ends and not leave the client with any unfinished emotional content or physical distress, such as light headedness or any other discomfort. This is also the time to thank the many energies and participants that interacted on behalf of the success of the session. Not only are you expressing gratitude—which raises the client's vibration—but you are also embedding the idea that the session has been successful. This helps those clients who later question themselves and the quality of their participation in the session, as some may think they didn't do well, because they were aware of their conscious mind throughout the entire session. They may have had the mistaken thought that they should have been completely knocked-out and unaware of what took place.

Imagine gift-wrapping a present with loving care, and tying the ribbon into a neat bow to create a beautiful presentation. Now imagine that the beginning of the session presented the mind-body lacking in congruence. Toward the middle of the session things got reshuffled, rejuvenated and harmonised beautifully into a congruent state. Now, at the end of the session, it's time to seal everything together, in order to ensure a calm and grounded confidence within your client. Without full completion the chances are reduced for any long-term results, and you may be sending the client away feeling emotionally fragile.

The ending of hypnosis is the time to incorporate more ego-strengthening suggestions to reinforce the client's confidence, positive self-regard, capabilities, and desire to learn and grow from the inside out. We all have within us everything needed to thrive and discover our self-value. It's important for us as practitioners to relight that flame of self-love and acceptance within our clients.

Reintegration, Auric Strengthening, and Grounding

On completion of the session if you don't reintegrate all parts of their energy it will be carried out automatically during the exit from trance, when you undertake their collective reintegration and request strengthening of the auric field to protect the work carried out during the session. These steps are particularly helpful for earthing or grounding any vibrational work that has been carried out.

During the pre-talk it may have been obvious that the client is in need of grounding, particularly if they don't like themselves much, aren't comfortable within themselves, are disassociated from their lives, or if they are in some emotional stress that makes it difficult to be fully present, as they are stuck in the past.

After any energy work the body needs to be grounded to prevent any healing crisis or physical discomfort from taking place. The client's own higher mind can guide them into the best ways to become and stay grounded, but additionally we can use some of the healing time to help them discover what they may need to do to support the work that began during the session. Grounding may mean the elimination or addition of dietary matters, being in nature in some way, or visualizing doing something like playing music or participating in a creative activity. Whatever it may take for an individual to become present, self aware, comfortable within their own skin, balanced and enjoying unconditional self acceptance, you as the practitioner must do whatever is necessary to accomplish this. Also, remind the client to follow any instructions that the SC recommends.

Recalibration of any restructured energy usually continues over the period of a few days after the session, as toxins are released and the body matrix is being grounded into place. This immediate time after the session is important—they need to be careful not to analyze or deconstruct what was recently rebuilt. This is one of the reasons why it is helpful to ask if an energetic protective shield can be placed around the client to help support the work that has been carried out. The shield adds a psychological, etheric, non-physical form of protection; not because there is a need to be protected from imagined fearful things, but to provide the client with a psychological tool for personal support. This is equivalent to erecting scaffolding to support a building while reconstruction work is underway. Clients need to leave the session grounded and fully present in the here and now, while the facilitator needs to stay grounded throughout the entire session.

Throughout the session, whenever positive character traits, energy expansion, valuable insights or wisdom are presented, this is a perfect time to invite the client to ground those positive experiences into their being. Opportunities to receive healing energy into the physical body will arise, so instruct the client to breathe those positive energies in at a deep cellular level—this allows all of their cells to reconnect, remember and absorb the traits in a unified way, which adds to the quality of their self-worth. The act of breathing positive experiences into the body subconsciously creates an integration of these aspects into the whole self. Taking action to do this is an intentional way of increasing inner focus, and this vibrational acceptance of increase is an easy way to integrate and embrace change without mental analysis.

When grounding healing energies into the physical body, suggest that the body knows what to do internally to create the easiest way to heal and integrate, and so there is no need to know how that will take place. Encourage the client to describe what is occurring, as well as to continue allowing the process to unfold at a deep level. This deters the mind from analyzing or blocking the process, and grounding the work ensures that it will be more likely to have lasting effects.

If, for example, work has been done in the solar plexus area, we can invite healing energies to also incorporate all the organs there, and include all the parts of the body that are connected to those organs. While that's being done we should ask, "Would the body benefit from an overall tune-up?" Once this has been completed ask that the: "Healing energy and the client's energy be anchored into the Earth, passing straight down into the core of the planet, to add the client's own unique signature or tone to the harmony of the planet, so the client will always know that she or he belongs here and can draw upon this energy anytime it is needed."

Taking precautions to resolve emotional discomforts, their impact on the body, and the beliefs or thoughts surrounding any disease or illness, is restorative for the body. This unity of consciousness will bridge the body-mind, which delivers even more insights to the client in the days following the session, as the mental, emotional and physical toxic residues dissolve and are released.

The completion of the session provides a time where things may be re-framed or discussed in a positive manner. The client must be allowed time to fully integrate back into the body, and become fully grounded within the body. They will feel relaxed and sometimes a little light-headed. It's important to offer them water and invite them to walk a little, if you have a garden that would be an ideal environment for this. The idea is to get them back into full present awareness.

Reintegration of all that has transpired energetically takes place, as full awareness is mindfully directed back into the present body, time and place. This process does take a while, and this time can be utilized to initiate some positive statements about their ability to continually expand in awareness. The client will be in an altered suggestible state for some minutes after the session has ended, and this is the perfect time to reaffirm ego strengthening by using post-hypnotic suggestion. There are times when the client may have experienced a life form that is non human. Effort should be made to bring their consciousness back integrated fully as a human. This I learned from a client who accessed a mermaid form being conscious of her body for a few days feeling as though her legs were restricted in some way that caused discomfort when walking.

Let the client know they will remember all of the session in their own way and time. Making this information available to the conscious mind provides them with choice and insight, which increases a long-term quality of self-awareness.

Key Words or Symbols:
Using KeyWords or Imagery to Re-Enter Hypnosis

It is important to realise that the keyword belongs TO the client and THEY put themselves back into trance. Wherever the key word or symbol is anchored will be a point of consciousness that they return to. It is like having a pin code to access a particular state of consciousness.

Symbols or significant images that are shown to the client at some point in hypnosis is often chosen. If, for example, they are with their soul group, guides, elders, light beings, or Source, then they use it to reconnect them back there easily.

Towards the end of the session and while they are still deeply relaxed you ask the client if they would like to re-enter their inner world easily. If you receive an affirmative answer, then ask them to give you a word(s), a symbol, shape or a colour that is meaningful for them to use.

When they say yes, you say:

"With your permission and only with your permission, each and every time I use the words__ __ you will immediately go back to this deep level of relaxation. You are always in control."

You repeat the key word to them and say:

"When I use this word, and only with your permission, you will achieve this beautiful, peaceful state of relaxation."

You can also add in deepeners at this point to have them go into an even deeper state of relaxation such as: "Each and every time I say this, you will relax even more and go deeper than you are now."

If you want to, use this for any following session(s), to save time by omitting the induction. Explain that the keyword/symbol will not work for others to access as they have no personal connection with them, and that hearing the words, or seeing the symbol, will not put them into trance unless they themselves have that intention. You can have them use it themselves to re-enter their trance before beginning your exploration. Once they enter their trance you might want to get their sensory abilities engaged by having them describe a setting, which could be their special place, wherever they left off in a previous session, or the starting point for a specific exploration. This sensory detailing works also as a deepener, switching off the external awareness while bringing the focus internally as it identifies a particular place, space or thing. Or you might simply say: "Go to wherever you need to be." Over time they will be able to access these levels of consciousness easily and quickly on their own; all that is needed is practice. I have numerous clients confirm to me that they have continued having an on-going dialogue with their 'higher self' through using their 'key'.

Self Hypnosis, and Meditation

During the post-talk, when clients are out of their formal trance and while they are still in an alpha/suggestible light trance state, I casually interrupt what we are talking about and say to them 'close your eyes and use your keyword, just repeat it in your mind and let it take you back into that space during your session where you discovered your symbol/words/color/etc.'

After their demonstration and when they open their eyes I discuss with them the benefits of using this to take themselves right into meditation or self hypnosis, explaining that it bypasses all the effort of trying to sit still or breathe deeply to settled down into a meditative state.

Why I do it casually during the post-talk is so clients don't engage their conscious mind to question or doubt whether they can do it or not. When I have them demonstrate this, I'll have them do so a few times to anchor it in its reality and efficacy, while boosting their confidence with their ability to be self-sufficient.

A Self-Hypnosis Script

This is a basic self-hypnosis script that can be modified to suit everyone's needs, and best demonstrated before exiting the session. Have them practise this during your post talk when they are still suggestible and confident in their ability to achieve trance.

Use the following method, saying something along the lines of 'you will find that you can access this state... again'.

Always get the permission of the higher mind to be able to be in further contact with what/who was initiated in the session. They never say no, but we ask anyhow to allow for a respectful communications grid to form and develop.

Say: "Countdown slowly 3...2...1 then close your eyes...the countdown is your subconscious cue to relax and alter your state each time you do it."

"Then think of symbol, a special place or something that gives you a nice feeling of pure love. Once this feeling is there, after a few moments, take your time initially, but after a while it will be instantaneous, open your eyes."

"Now that you are mentally relaxed, close your eyes. I like to close my eyes, and focus on relaxing around the eyes until my eyelids are pleasantly heavy and then deliberately send that feeling of relaxation down to my toes a few times, enjoying the waves of relaxation coursing through my body." This is distracting for the left brain while giving the conscious mind something to observe, which quietens it and makes it step back from further activity.

This following step can be used with your clients at the end of their session. Say to them while they are still very suggestible:

1. Think of your personal symbol or image (or special place) and associate with the feeling it gives you, feeling it deeply in your cellular structure - have them do this about 3 times to build on the feeling each time. "increase the feeling of...and enjoy the...it gives you"

2. Now count yourself down 3 2 1 and you instantly go back to this deep relaxed state you're in now.

3. You can choose how long or short you stay there and when you like to exit this place then mentally count up 1 2 3 and open your eyes and you'll become fully aware in present time. If any emergency happens around you, you'll become fully aware and deal with it, for example, if the house is on fire... this allows them the confidence to know that they are still able to be effective in their environment.

4. Now bring them back to present time... this is also a good time to get a keyword as they are deeply entranced and this is a state you would like them to be in for future work...On the count of 5 you'll open your eyes and be fully aware and alert.

5. Then have the client demonstrate that they can do this by going back into trance, because of the fractionation of opening and closing their eyes they will do so easily which gives them and their conscious mind the confidence to achieve this at home.

6. Say to them: "Whenever you use this method you will go deeper each time and it is recommended you do this once or twice a day... and the more you use this technique the more benefit you achieve from this method... focusing on one objective at a time... just create

the image that you want to achieve and your subconscious mind will make that a reality as it knows the best way to achieve this... everybody knows that our subconscious mind works in miraculous ways... etc., etc."

When we keep asking them to put themselves back into trance to practice their ability, they are compounding their trance state, achieving deeper states each time. We can use self-hypnosis to refine and improve on any area, or skills and outcomes in our lives.

Post-Hypnotic Suggestions

Amnesia

Although amnesia is a natural phenomena of hypnosis we can use it to our advantage when instilling post-hypnotic suggestions to think less about the past, as the client is now fully focused on their present. This is especially effective for moving away from trauma or physical illness, as the mind will now be focused on creating more expansive ideas and perceptions. We can never force anyone to go deeply into their buried past, but we can help them in the present time to move ahead. There will be no need to reconnect with past feelings, as the problems will no longer be there and this will eliminate the mental need for excessive analysis. It is possible to bypass many unnecessary doubts that may occur later by hypnotically planting the seed that they: "Will feel better than ever before, and they will feel surprised and amazed at how good they continue to feel, increasingly so in the days and weeks to come." Never allude to any kind of negative future feelings, as anything you say will act as a post-hypnotic command to be experienced.

Bringing the Client Back to Full Conscious Awareness

It's important to seal the ending of the session in such a way that full awareness becomes fully present in the body and mind. This will lighten the trance state, bringing the focus back up from the depths that have been explored. Consciousness is focused wherever awareness is directed with full attention, making it important to have the client fully grounded and back into their current life personality.

You can creatively provide them with guidance to bring them back into full awareness, feeling alert and feeling better than before. This can also be applied if they suddenly open their eyes or sit up, by gently suggesting that they lie back down or close their eyes, and inhale deeply. As they exhale slowly they will either go back into deep relaxation, or if it is the end of the session you can instead let them know that you are going to count them up, out and back into full conscious awareness. Ideally it's preferable to mention during post-hypnotic suggestions how increasingly well they will feel.

Post-Hypnotic Markers

Post-Hypnotic Markers are pointers that should be mentioned to help support the CM in accepting what has transpired without having any doubts. Because they might have felt at times not deeply entranced and so can remember things, does not mean that they will remember everything. The brainwaves would have naturally fluctuated between many states ranging from low and high alpha or theta, at times dipping into delta or gamma. Perhaps they remember hearing cars going by on the street outside, but not hearing a baby crying at another time.

Once having gone into an expansion of consciousness, opening new neural pathways, then there is a good chance that the mind will think differently. The deep relaxation also adds its benefit in leaving the mind/body/spirit more relaxed and calmer. Below are some of the markers that may be noticed to confirm the veracity of having been hypnotised.

1. Fragmented memories or amnesia.
2. Willingness to accept new ideas or approaches.
3. Greater sense of well being and purpose.
4. Renewed confidence and strengthened ego or sense of self.

Anchoring Positive Feelings

A pleasant, supportive post-talk and closure of the session is just the beginning of the client's experience that they will take out into their world. Use this opportunity to persuade the client to follow the guidance suggested by their higher mind. We don't overtly tell them what to do, but instead encourage willingness in the client to do what is needed for themselves. The post-talk should be designed to tie everything together with enthusiasm, insight and an upbeat tempo, to anchor in place a positive conclusion. Remember that the client is still hypnotically suggestible, so this is a good time to anchor in the positive feelings that occurred during the session and provide meaningful closure.

Never tell them it is up to them to heal themselves, as this creates in their mind the idea of willpower, which always presupposes an internal battle with the need to suppress and overcome via the will. Willpower encourages ideas of struggle and a lack of natural ability. What better opportunity than when they are still suggestible to affirm and inspire? They will be in an alpha brainwave state, and easily able to be receptive while having full awareness of their body-mind too.

Anything discussed at this time is absorbed deeply, so it is important that we only communicate in positive ways, as their subconscious will pick out the negative thoughts or words and make them seem more important than you may have meant them to be. Learning how to phrase your ideas in a positive light is crucial throughout all of your communications. Anything said now becomes a post-hypnotic suggestion and an embedded command that the client's mind will act on.

If they accessed new feelings of love (or any other positive feeling) then casually say: "Close your eyes and feel that feeling of love again, and when you do just say yes." They easily reconnect with this — which confirms to them that they have this feeling of love inside and can reconnect with what is already there any time. Remind them that they identified in the pre-talk that they would like more love, they experienced it during hypnosis, and now they can revisit those feelings, as well as know how to bring love into all aspects of their life.

It was brought to my attention by many clients' SCs that it's important for them to remember everything that occurred during hypnosis, because the knowledge disclosed will release more spontaneous information in later downloads. They also stressed that we are now in a newer expression of energy on the planet, which creates more alignment between the conscious, subconscious and higher conscious, allowing for a more direct communication. We can give a post-hypnotic suggestion that they will remember everything that occurred.

The ultimate aim is to have the clients leave feeling highly motivated to continue what began in their session. We want them to feel a greater connection with their multidimensional inner-world, and find new enthusiasm for themselves and their lives. What is initiated in the session begins the changes effortlessly, as the SC works in natural and seamless ways.

Restating Main Ideas

Effectively, what we do in the post-talk is restate the main ideas expressed by their own consciousness in the session, and emphasise how this has been fixed by what was said or done. Finding from the client what their feelings or insights were about the session provides information that we can reinforce, while also adding our insights to seed additional ways of thinking, seeing or interpreting the information. We restate the main ideas brought forward to emphasise how things have been fixed or expressed and to share our thoughts on what was suggested.

Some of this may seem to be new information, as the client may not remember much or anything that transpired in the session, depending on their depth of trance. Some information may take a week, a month, a year or even two years before the meaning becomes clear, as this is an on-going process.

Since they are still in a suggestible state of mind, it is very simple to make open-ended suggestions, said with warmth and charm and stated as fact, for example: "You will find that it will be an on-going desire of your subconscious mind or higher self to inspire you in little ways, to take action for your physical transformation. You will notice the ideas will just come to you in so many ways, just like being guided to do and find what you need at any given time." We can share ideas and examples of how others have found success with the methods suggested, by using truisms and storytelling.

As an observer we may notice connections that were not obvious to the client. We always add our insights as merely possibilities, not as absolutes, as we remind the client that they will make sense of their own experience in ways we cannot. Hypnosis pioneer, Dr. Milton Erickson, popularised the technique of using storytelling metaphors with similar themes to whatever the presenting problems are. I find that it's really helpful to adopt this style, by prefacing these creative 'stories' by saying something like, "I once knew (or heard of) a lady/man who...," allowing the mind to process how it can also accomplish what others have done. Remember the SC will naturally personalise resonant information, and will find its own meaning in relation to them.

Addressing Problems in the Session

One of the post-hypnotic suggestions that I use—which ensures a positive on-going outcome (whether they listen to their recording or not), does not reduce the efficacy of the work, and addresses any blips in the session—is something along the lines of: "Even though you felt there was no response to... (add the query), in actuality, having now opened that computer file storing that information within your subconscious, you will, over time, notice that those answers will just naturally flow into your daily life by encouraging and shifting your perspectives and actions, and only in hindsight will you realise those connections to this session," or something similar. This follows on from ideas mentioned in the pre-talk, that the mind-brain is like a computer that has all the stored knowledge about them and their lives, and when they ask questions it's like opening a computer file that stores all information on the topic. Remember that they are still under the influence of hypnosis and ANYTHING you say to them acts as a post-hypnotic embedded command. The SC has a way of bringing clients into their spiritual essence effortlessly, and in a way that they can accept.

Post-Session Discomfort

After sessions clients have asked why they felt a pulling sensation at the crown of their heads, or why they felt pressure at the centre of their forehead, which may still feel uncomfortable—in fact they often mention this during the session. If this occurs, gently have them close their eyes, use their keyword or symbol to reconnect with their inner world, and have them fully ground back into their body. It may be that there is a need for further healing to relieve those feelings. Remember that hypnosis is used for pain relief; this should give you confidence that you can help clients to remove discomfort.

Providing Support and Aftercare Advice

Asking the client's permission to share relevant information and supporting information with them always receives an enthusiastic response. These might be the work of authors, scientific information, dietary suggestions, or any relevant information that will add insight or collaboration to what has transpired during the sessions.

In this way you are helping to further their education and you have not crossed any boundaries by judging that they are lacking in some way, or by telling them what they need or what they should be doing. A good deal of information will have already been shared during the pre-talk, so take mental notes about additional reference material that may be of help to them later. Keep information on hand on various topics, such as consciousness exploration and expansion, grounding, dietary material, breathwork, muscle testing, space clearing, neuroscience, archetypal energies, quantum research, hemi-sync music, and an even wider range of subjects that support higher consciousness and quality mind-body-spirit integration materials.

Remind clients that:

1) Hypnosis creates a natural interactive brain state, which creates a harmonious flow between the left and right hemispheres, switching on their own self-healing forces to bring health and wellbeing back into equilibrium. This relaxed feeling will continue for a number of days. They may sleep deeply and restfully the night after the session and have vivid dreams, which is a continuation of the interaction between the different levels of your consciousness. This is the process of creating natural effortless changes in their life to match their personal desires. It is helpful to begin keeping a journal if they do not already do so.

2) Resist questioning whether they imagined or made up the information during the session. Instead, use the following days to see how this connects to the reasons they sought out this direct communication with their own subconscious. Whether the information revealed was an analogy, metaphor, symbolic or a subliminal reality, stay open-minded and allow the insights to continue downloading, and they will see how the dots connect with their life as they were experiencing it.

3) Give themselves the time and space to reflect on and process what has transpired. Observe this taking place, as their energetic clearing, healing and detox will be on-going for a number of days. They have had a unique experience of inter-communication with other aspects of their consciousness, and this inner-dialogue will be on-going. The quantum effects taking place during the session will restore or initiate new neural brain patterns, so expect more intuitive and spontaneous thoughts and knowings — the session was just the beginning.

4) Drinking lots of water is highly recommended to rid the body and flush the system of the many toxins released through this deep energy and self-healing work. The benefits of water as a cleansing aid can be utilised even more when they shower with the intent of deeply cleansing all subtle energy bodies, or by using a handful of salt in their bath water.

5) Spend a moment each day in gratitude for the physical healing and consciousness shift that has taken place. Also include appreciation for their body's ability

to heal itself. Gratitude moves them into the heart, which supports the healing process in the very best way possible. They will receive the most benefit if their participation is coupled with the intention to heal. The overall best results will occur if they follow the guidance that they themselves have provided throughout the session, through the direct communication with their own SC and higher self.

6) Listening to the recording of the session will increase the effectiveness of any healing that took place. It will also allow a continuation of downloads and an expansion of awareness as they revisit those levels of consciousness. There is always more taking place during the session that remains unspoken, as they only answered the questions asked. When revisiting the session they are able to return to the state of consciousness that was previously accessed, hence they can gather even more wisdom and knowledge.

Providing complementary support helps in a way that friends and family might not be able to. Sometimes clients are isolated with their new outlook, because friends and family may lack understanding or insight. Providing a source of support that your clients can relate to is important, and aftercare advice is also genuinely appreciated. Suggest that they maintain their connection with their higher mind by regular use of self-hypnosis or meditation, this way they can revisit their own support system any time they choose.

A session story:
The Auditorium, Yoda, and Earth Volunteers

There are repetitive themes and patterns that run

through all of our experiences. An example of a popular one is the Missionary soul archetype that consist of 'volunteers,' who enter or incarnate within different reality systems to help and aid others in some way. The following story is just one such example:

Natalie was worried she would not be able to be hypnotised or connect with her higher self—but she needn't have been at all concerned, the information flowed non-stop! Yet I was surprised when she accessed the scene of an auditorium and a call for volunteers for Earth.

After her past-life experience I guide her to the death scene and she finds herself floating upwards towards a light, feeling very warm and happy. Her voice and demeanour soften with an ecstatic feeling of breathlessness, as she describes the different layers she moves through, with accompanying feelings and a vibrational humming: "I'm in a ray going up towards the light, which is like the sun. The light pulls me in and I'm surrounded by pink and gold light. I'm going to rest, the light is me and I'm connected to all light. There are other specks of light too, and that is also what I am. I will stay here for a while to work out what my next move will be."

I tell her that time has speeded up and she now knows what she will do next. "It's hard to think as I'm just being and it's nice. I never want to leave this place, but I will when I have to and when I'm needed." I tell her that I wonder if she can leave a part of herself there in the light and move on to find out what is needed, and we can come back to connect and integrate with that part. She agrees.

She now finds herself in space surrounded by rocks

that look almost 'fake and very vivid.' She finds herself in a spaceship contraption, and needs some time to understand this, so I suggest that we compress time. She discovers there is another man in the ship who shape-shifts into different forms. (This later evolves to show her that, as an energy being, she can shape-shift to different forms of beings and places she goes to, so she can fit in.) They are on a mission together to save a planet. They are not right for this planet and that is why they have the ability to change form. In this case the energy of the planet is wrong. (She explains that this affects her coping skills in her current life, as she is so sensitive to others.) She is androgynous and moves through an atmosphere that is 'gaseous and pink' and feels like she is falling down. They are now on the planet to send love, and there are others who are doing the same. That is why it is pink, "because of the love there."

She tells me that others are doing the same work: "They look human but they are not dense. They are a lighter human, almost transparent looking. The people are beautiful and there is a lot of beauty on the planet, and I don't even know why it needs saving." I tell her to take a deep breath and as she exhales she will know why. As she does so she tells me that: "It was on the cusp of going the other way, and lots of people have come in and are just existing here so it has shifted it. It happened at a crucial time before things got too difficult to change, the potential was spotted in advance this time." When I ask if it has happened before she replies: "Loads of times, LOADS of times, and when it's not spotted in time it's a really hard task to turn it back, and no matter how many people you send it can take a long time—like millions of years—and sometimes it isn't successful. This time is a really good time, one of the better occasions." As the information flows she realises that she knows the other person who came with her to be a great friend, but from another existence. They've done this work on other planetary systems so she knows it's effective and she can do it, besides she's not alone as there are many others doing the same.

I ask her if she can locate the planning stage of coming into life here at this time. She tells me: "We are all called…we all arrive together and it happens in different phases, as we all come at different times. Those who are to come at similar times all come together at the same time, like group energy, and it's fed and imprinted into them what is needed. They just get it. They have to go down a few levels to people who are already there, to work out how and what we are going to do. It's not that we are going to change the world, but it's the subtle changes that are needed and the vibrations…wherever we are when we are needed we get a calling and we just know. No-one really talks to you, you just know and understand, as it's to do with the senses. It's like a pink light calls us and we come in, and it could look like we are in the equivalent of a courthouse…inside it's like a conference place." I ask if it's like an auditorium: "Yes and it's nice because you see everyone. They come in different forms: light, shapes, blobs, creatures, and transparent beings that look like gaseous humans." I ask if anyone is in charge. "Yeah, a big, big creature, and he's lovely, but he doesn't look lovely so if he were down here people would be running for their lives. I feel wisdom from him; he's like a bigger Yoda. He's a bit browner, more wrinkled, and like nothing that I can describe, he has little ankles and feet with a big round dense body. He doesn't speak but his eyes are big. He's the spokesperson for the more knowledgeable greater power, who is the controlling body for the universe. Everyone is now told the situation, so let's start making the plans."

She is part of a large group, it's one of many, and there is still a lot of work that to be done. She recognises some of her friends in her current life and familiar people that she may meet if their paths cross. They know what they need to do and go to do it: "My assignment is to be love, and it's hard because when I'm here on the planet not everyone thinks the same, you're seen as weak and you don't get to know boundaries. It can make me feel empty, fragile and like there is a hole inside." When I ask if there is something factored in to help her she says: "I have a team — we all have — that come to me in my dreams. Sometimes they scare me at night but they don't mean to." I ask if it's possible to meet the team now.

We have a long discussion with them regarding her questions and they give her healing. She even describes them individually and explains why they are on the team. Interestingly, one man has wings and he is there to protect her when she gives light and love and he "steers her in the right direction." She cannot pronounce his name as it sounds like ancient Greek. I ask her if they have a message for her but she does not understand it, so I tell her to breathe deeply and allow it to just become a part of her energy field.

The team tell her: "When she is not listening to her soul and heart, then she gets frustrated and her power is taken away. Also we connect to her during meditation and download ideas, trust instinct as it is always right, you don't trust it enough. You need to push the thoughts of others out of your head and create a bubble, so you can focus on your own thoughts, and what you really want from your heart, follow that." They also tell her about finding her own rhythm and they are going to help her by "tuning her up", and she describes this as it takes place, it will be an "on-going gradual process."

To me it sounded like psychic surgery: making incisions, removing balls, blockages and 'energetic barbed wires.' They open incisions and after removing things close them again. This is not, "just from this life but all the lives, because when we leave life and come back it doesn't matter what existence we come back to, all the same patterns or injuries will come back if they haven't been released."

Regarding her weight issues, she is to: "Eat natural, eat simply and don't overeat as it stresses out my body because it is different from normal bodies, because I'm lighter and I find it hard being dense here. I don't need as much food or drink as other people and I shouldn't listen to government guidelines about what I should or shouldn't eat. If I eat more than I should, I overload my body and have intolerances. I'm just to naturally graze and everything will be fine." (Strangely, another client said a similar thing recently too.) "Because I have not been in human form for a long time I can't deal with the denseness. I got out of my rhythm as a baby because people couldn't understand me being different to them, as I found it hard to adjust to being in a human body." This has affected her whole life.

In Natalie's pre-talk she recalled her mother saying she was very sick during the pregnancy, would hear voices and feel dead from the feet up. "My mum's preeclampsia was because I really didn't want to come. In the end they induced me as I had second thoughts," she laughs, "and was thinking, do I want to go back? So my energy was coming in and out and causing my mum issues, and she found it so difficult with all the voices she heard. This was because she was tapping into some of the conferences, and my coming and going would keep changing her energy. I was a bit tricky because I wasn't sure, but once I came and stayed in the womb, I felt comfortable and didn't want to come out. Even though the induction was at the right time I would have stayed in the womb longer if I could have."

She had this to say about death: "I know that death is nothing to fear now…it actually feels pretty amazing, better than birth. Birth is scary, it is a rush, and you go from being an active soul to a little body that cannot function. When you die you float, you bounce and you go back to love."

RECOMMENDED BOOKS

The Secret of the Soul: Using Out-of-Body Experiences to Understand Our True Nature: William Buhlman

Akashic Experience: Science and the Cosmic Memory Field: Ervin Laszlo

Awakening the Mind: A Guide to Mastering the Power of Your Brain Waves: A Guide of Mastering the Power of Your Brain Waves: Anna Wise

The New Regression Therapy: Healing the Wounds and Trauma of This Life and Past Lives with the Presence and Light Of The Divine: Greg McHugh CCHt

My Voice Will Go with You: Teaching Tales of Milton H. Erickson: Sidney Rosen

Past Life Therapy in Action: Dick Sutphen

Your Soul's Gift: Robert Schwartz

Soul Retrieval: Mending the Fragmented Self: Sandra Ingerman

Voices from the Womb: Adults Re-live Their Pre-birth Experiences: Michael Gabriel

Afterlife Knowledge Guidebook: A Manual for the Art of Retrieval and Afterlife Exploration (Exploring the Afterlife): Bruce Moen

Adventures in the Afterlife: Volume 1: William Buhlman

Life Before Life: Helen Wambach

Vistas of Infinity - How to Enjoy Life When You Are Dead: Jurgen Ziewe

An Amazing Human Journey: Remembering from the Subconscious Mind, Volume Two Paperback: M.D. Shakuntala Modi

Hypnosis and the Higher Self Hardcover: Lawrence Follas

Encounters: Edith Fiore

Journey of Souls: Case Studies of Life Between Lives: Michael Newton